The Mountain Bike Leader's Handbook

Graham French

First published 2017

Copyright © Graham French 2017

Graham French, has exerted the right to be identified as the author of this work in accordance with sections 77 and 78 of the Copyright, Designs and Patents Act 1988.

All rights reserved. No part of this book may be reprinted or reproduced or utilised in any form or by any electronic, mechanical or other means, now known or hereafter invented, including photocopying and recording, or in any information storage or retrieval system, without permission in writing from the author.
Trademark notice: Product or corporate names may be trademarks or registered trademarks, and are only used for identification, exemplification and explantation without intent to infringe.

For all enquiries please contact: graham@agoadventures.co.uk

Photos - Cover: The Long Mynd, Shropshire
Title page: Jonny rides the Marin trail, North Wales
This page: A windswept Upper Burbage Bridge car park, Peak District

The Mountain Bike Leader's Handbook

Graham French

Contents

Photo credits	iii
Foreword	viii
Acknowledgements	ix
Introduction	1
1. Leadership	2
2. Coaching	18
3. Environmental Impact	40
4. Access	48
5. Riding skills	60
6. Navigation	92
7. What to Carry	110
8. Know Your Bike	120
9. First Aid	136
10. Conclusion	146

Photo/Image credits

Unless otherwise stated below, all photos are from the author and as such all rights are reserved for those images. Other credits appear below. All other images have not been modified and are used under the Creative commons license, details of which can be found here: https://creativecommons.org/licenses/by/2.0/

piii+iv - Mountain biking, John O'Nolan - used under Creative commons license - original at: http://tinyurl.com/gvwbr53

pv+vi - Coed-y-Brenin, BkMSE - used under Creative commons license - original at: http://tinyurl.com/h4dz7v3

pv+vi Foreword - Yet another Yeti shot, Zach Dischner - used under Creative commons license - original at: http://tinyurl.com/jb7yzcp

p21 photo 2.1 - 3-9-12: Direction, Emily Mills - used under Creative commons license - original at: http://tinyurl.com/grhjkq6

p39 end of chapter 2 - Pump track - Nathaniel, Jack Flanagan - sed under Creative commons license - original at: http://tinyurl.com/zuv55xa

p40+41 Chapter 3. Environmental impact - chapter page - Uncle Fester, Red Craig - used under Creative commons license - original at: http://tinyurl.com/jufkuqh

p43 photo 3.1 - Footpath erosion near Coire Cas, Jim McDougall - used under Creative commons license - original at: http://tinyurl.com/zjuoksz

p44 photo 3.2 - Braking bumps, MattGoesSomewhere - used under Creative commons license - original at: http://tinyurl.com/zcgjwfd

p45 photo 3.3 - IMG_3087, Hugh Lunnon - used under Creative commons license - original at: http://tinyurl.com/hr9ojhc

p47 photo 3.4 - Toad stool, Red Craig - used under Creative commons license - original at: http://tinyurl.com/zgkxbfd

p48+49 Chapter 4. Access - chapter page - Signpost, Artengill, Colin

Gregory - used under Creative commons license - original at: http://tinyurl.com/gqtdazd

p53 Figure 4.1 -Section from Ordnance Survey Outdoor Leisure 1 The Peak district -Dark Peak Area used by permission OS licence no. 100058331 © Crown copyright 1998

p52+53 Coed Llandegla Forest - Blue & Red Climb, William Hook - used under Creative commons license - original at: http://tinyurl.com/zd522wl

p55 photo 4.2 - Beast trailhead map, Red Craig - used under Creative commons license - original at: http://tinyurl.com/z6xcwm3

p59 photo 4.3 - Brechfa, BkMSE - used under Creative commons license - original at: http://tinyurl.com/h5tvr4c

p59 photo 4.4 - Coed Llandegla (2), robocup2009 - used under Creative commons license - original at: http://tinyurl.com/jpcec29

p83 photo 5.9 - Eyes to the exit, Tom Grundy Photo - used under Creative commons license - original at: http://tinyurl.com/zbjxb44

p92 Chapter 6. Navigation - chapter page - Compass, Jonny Kreidler - used under Creative commons license - original at: http://tinyurl.com/hcge6vt

p95 photo 6.1 - Long distance, Andrew Gustar - used under Creative commons license - original at: http://tinyurl.com/hp28eah

p100 photo 6.3 - Compass confusion, henrikjon - used under Creative commons license - original at: http://tinyurl.com/zbsl6qf

p106 photo 6.4 - Uncle Fester, Red Craig - used under Creative commons license - original at: http://tinyurl.com/jufkuqh

p106 photo 6.4 - GOC Wild Beds and Edgy Herts 085: Access, Peter O'Connor aka anem...used under Creative commons license - original at: http://tinyurl.com/gocztxq

p106 photo 6.4 - Choices, Peter O'Connor aka anem... - used under Creative commons license - original at: http://tinyurl.com/jhyul9s

p109 end of chapter photo - Single track mountain bike, Mark Turner -

used under Creative commons license - original at: http://tinyurl.com/h548um7

p114 photo 7.4 - Bike chain and chain tool on the ground, Andrea Kambanis - used under Creative commons license - original at: http://tinyurl.com/hly9yrh

p116 photo 7.7 - First aid kit, DLG Images - used under Creative commons license - original at: http://tinyurl.com/h5q5caz

p116 photo 7.8 - IMG_2114, Joe Loong - used under Creative commons license - original at: http://tinyurl.com/hr6f8lv

p118 end of chapter 7 - Antur Stiniog - 4th September 2014, William Hook - original at: http://tinyurl.com/z6bvtak

p124 photo 8.1 - Giant Glory Advanced 1, Pushbikes NZ - used under Creative commons license - original at: http://tinyurl.com/ha6327g

p125 photo 8.2 - IMG_4196, maplegirlie - used under Creative commons license - original at: http://tinyurl.com/ztwpdv9

p125 photo 8.3 - Santa Cruz Nomad C, David Lienhard - used under Creative commons license - original at: http://tinyurl.com/gtpkzd4

p126 photo 8.4 - Rocky Mountain Vertex, Dustin Gaffke used under Creative commons license - original at: http://tinyurl.com/jqou3e9

p128 photo 8.8 - Avid BB7 Front, Jeff Attaway - used under Creative commons license - original at: http://tinyurl.com/zyc25j4

p129 photo 8.9 - A Pedal, Bill Selak - used under Creative commons license - original at: http://tinyurl.com/hmuy689

p129 photo 8.9 - Japtech, JKW - used under Creative commons license - original at: http://tinyurl.com/hvnuqm8

p?129 photo 8.9 - Flat pedals rock, Beth H - used under Creative commons license - original at: http://tinyurl.com/jxy4f4z

p130 photo 8.11 - Niner 29er Carbon Fork w. 15mm Thru Axle, Glory Cycles - used under Creative commons license - original at: http://tinyurl.com/z8lltyr

p131 photo 8.12 - Burnside lake snow ride, Jeff Moser - used under Creative commons license - original at: http://tinyurl.com/zjukafd

p132 - end of chapter photo - Flat tyre and terrain, Mr Hicks46 - used under Creative commons license - original at: http://tinyurl.com/j3cpy5s

p142 photo 9.4 - Matt_Clare-X-Ray_IMG00002, Matt Clare - used under Creative commons license - original at: http://tinyurl.com/zjvqru8

p150 Index page - DSCF6243, Hunny Alrohaif - used under Creative commons license - original at: http://tinyurl.com/humponm

Mountain biking is a hazardous and dangerous activity. Every care has been taken by the author in compilation of the information contained herein and in verification of its accuracy when published, however the content of this guidebook is subject to change without notice due to factors outside the control of the author and this book should, therefore, be used as a guide only.

This book is published and distributed on the basis that the publisher and author are not responsible for the results of any actions taken by users of information contained in this book, on the basis of information contained in this book nor for any error in or omission from this book. The author does not accept any responsibility whatsoever for misrepresentation by any person whatsoever of the information contained in this book and expressly disclaims all and any liability and responsibility to any person, whether a reader of this book or not, in respect of claims, losses or damage or any other matter, either direct or consequential arising out of or in relation to the use and reliance, whether wholly or partially, upon any information contained or products referred to in this book.

The Mountain Bike Leader's Handbook

Foreword

When I first started teaching mountain bike skills some years ago, I wanted a reference manual to give me the top tips and handy hints to allow me to lead a group of students effectively. I came from a background of paddlesport coaching and mountaineering, where there are quite a lot of books written about leading and coaching effectively. I was disappointed to find this was not the case with mountain biking, but after a long hard look, decided I'd just have to work things out for myself. Articles in magazines informed and inspired me to get better, but I wondered how anyone was supposed to know how to teach this stuff.

Fast forward 10 years and when I started work training teachers working in outdoor activities, they too wanted something to look at and refer to for some post-course revision. When I began delivering mountain bike leadership awards through MIAS, I was challenged to think and work hard to produce resources that would effectively support learners in my leadership courses. I started out with some slide shows based on the syllabi for the awards, and then produced a DVD of the sections of the syllabus I most needed support in delivering. I moved with the times and now have a YouTube channel devoted to such resources in video form. I still felt however that there was something missing

from the resource base and I was repeating myself frequently in the resources I created. Finally, after years of delay and prevarication, I got round to putting fingers to keyboard, collecting together all the best bits of the resources I've made over the years and trying to turn them into a reference manual for a an aspirant mountain bike leader. This is the volume you are about to embark on, and I hope it is useful and informative and inspires you to get out and share your mountain bike adventures.

Happy riding

Graham

The Mountain Bike Leader's Handbook

Acknowledgements

I'm very lucky to have been able to ride a bike from a young age, and grown up in a time and place where I could go out to the woods with friends for whole days during school holidays and learn and play at the same time. Memories of building jumps and finding stuff other lads had already built in the woods still bring a smile to my face.

I was fortunate to go to university in Bangor, and so had a national park right on my doorstep, and for all the time I've lived in North Wales I've ridden in the mountains, woods and along the coast.

Thanks to my dad for getting me that first bike, teaching me to ride it and look after it, and then letting me go off and explore. Thanks also to my family who have put up with all the times I've been sat in front of a computer writing and not out riding my bike with them!

Finally thanks to the guys who've helped with the photos as models (Jonny, Tom, George, Paul, Simon, Steve and all the former students of NCT), and especially to my wife Julie.

Introduction

With the increasing popularity of mountain biking as a fun, healthy, recreational activity, there are more and more beginners and intermediate riders out there looking to improve their skills and discover adventure.

Enter the mountain bike leader.

But where did they learn how to lead, encourage, coach, and repair? This book aims to support the development of those aspiring to lead, or improve their leadership of, mountain biking groups. It provides a resource to be consulted as necessary, or read as a complete volume of advice and guidance. It is not a substitute for going on a MTB leader training course!

It's not a manual of mountain bike skills, riding technique, navigation or first aid. But it does cover all those things and more, and attempts to tie the mountain bike specific bits of all these topics into one easily digestible volume, where answers to common questions can be found.

See you on the trail!

1. Leadership

> So what does a leader actually do? What are the qualities, roles and responsibilities of a leader? This chapter aims to give an overview at the start of the book and a context for each of the other chapters. It also describes and defines what is meant by the term leadership, within mountain biking.

Beddgelert Forest, Snowdonia

Leadership

It seems appropriate for a handbook for a mountain bike leader to start off by looking at what leadership and being a leader are all about. There are many facets to being a leader and many reasons for wanting to lead and this opening chapter will aim to give the fundamental roles and responsibilities of a leader, and also look at how to be a good leader in a mountain biking context.

Primarily, a question to ask yourself is 'Why should anyone be led by me?' The answer to this question may be as simple as 'I am the most experienced/skilled/qualified rider amongst a group so it falls to me'. It may be that you are working for a provider or have been engaged as a guide/coach by a group who want an adventure or to develop their mountain biking skills. Rarely will people follow a leader because of a title or perceived position of responsibility, so if you want to be a successful leader it is important to understand more of what actually contributes to effective leadership.

Putting some of the psychology associated with understanding leadership into a mountain biking context is important so that it is not lost in a change of context. Much has been written on leadership in a sporting context, as well as a more general business management orientated approach, but there are some specific things that only apply to adventure sports leadership such as mountain biking, not least the potentially hazardous nature of the activity we are leading.

Roles of a leader

A leader is someone who leads, right? But what do they do as part of that process? Leaders act as teachers and coaches when technical skill development is required. Leaders act as mentors when riders are learning how to do things and need an example to follow. Leaders act as guides when their group doesn't know which way to go (both physically and metaphorically) and leaders make decisions where others can't or choose not to.

So, as a leader you need to be prepared to fulfil each of these roles at certain times, sometimes decided by you in advance and sometimes necessitated by circumstance. It is therefore important to consider how to act in each situation, and to do that you need to understand the different styles of leadership.

Styles of leadership

When I first taught about leadership theory it was to a group of BTEC Outdoor Education students at an FE college, and the syllabus quite clearly stated they had to be taught about autocratic, democratic and abdicratic leadership. As I learned more about these styles (and what the words actually meant!) I realised that this was a simple picture which didn't really explain or fit with many of the situations adventure sports leaders are faced with. (Just to clear up the meanings - autocratic leaders are usually seen as directive leaders who make all the decisions and give the orders, democratic leaders ask for a group opinion and then make decisions based on a consensus view, and abdicratic leaders just let the group get on with it - also know as a laissez faire style).

> **Top Tip:**
> Play to your strengths - use the styles of leadership you feel most comfortable with and find most effective. Only experiment with a new style if you feel the absolute need to change what you do. The old adage 'if it ain't broke, don't fix it' rings true about leadership. It's far harder to be authentic by trying to use a style which you don't understand, see the reason for or find really difficult to do. In order to be authentic stick with what you know. Authenticity is far more important in being an effective leader than looking good or ticking a leadership style box.

Understanding that there are in fact more styles than this helps us not only appreciate our strengths as leaders but also the overlap between styles gives us tools to solve leadership problems - be they inter-relational (group management), physical (risk management), psychological (expectation management) or anything else.

One of the most important aspects of being a leader, identified by many authors, is to be authentic. Of the list of leadership styles set out in figure 1.1 there are likely to one or two that you are comfortable with either because you have experience in using this style or it naturally comes from your personality and experiences. There will be others you are either totally unfamiliar with or feel incapable of using.

The style you use or chose to use may be planned or spur-of-the-moment depending on the situation and your experience. An experienced leader can switch between styles to match the situation as there are different types of scenario that are best (but not only) suited to a particular style. For instance, if a group member is riding too fast and you can see they will not be able stop or avoid an obstacle you may be directive to shout instructions for them to brake or steer. Clearly a consensus style would be inappropriate. However, if you were leading a group of peers on a club or 'mates' ride, being directive may well make you pretty unpopular, so a consensus or affiliative style would be more appropriate then.

Responsibilities of a leader

As a leader you have in some way, either through direct decision (being employed as a mountain bike leader) or unconscious allocation of role (you are the more experienced of a group of riders out for a ride together) gained a degree of responsibility for the group you are riding with. If you have completed any training in mountain bike leadership then you also have a duty of care to the people you are riding with, as a more experienced and educated individual (in the context of mountain biking).

Some responsibilities will come with a specific allocation of role - if you have been engaged as a guide you clearly have responsibilities for show-

Directive leaders	Demanding compliance and obedience with rules
Engaged leaders	Mobilising people around shared values and purpose
Coaching leaders	Developing people for leadership roles
Consensus leaders	Building agreement through participation
Affiliative leaders	Creating emotional bonds and harmony
Expert leaders	Expecting competence and self-direction

Figure 1.1: Leadership styles (adapted from True North, by Bill George pp190-192)

ing a group of individuals the way to go to have an enjoyable adventure on their bikes. If you have been asked to coach a group and develop specific technical skills then you need to accept the responsibilities of developing each rider's skills as much as possible in the time you are working with them.

There are a number of generic responsibilities which a leader takes on, by accepting the mantle of leadership, and it is important to bear these in mind at all times. As a leader you have to be aware of, and do all you reasonably can to ensure, your group's safety, and to a lesser extent (but still important) other trail users or members of the public in the area where you're riding. You have a responsibility to the environment in which you ride to have as little impact as possible on it (see chapter 3). You have responsibility for the enjoyment and well-being of the group you are leading, and to a lesser extent you have a responsibility to develop their skills, be that technical, social interaction or navigation. The safety of your group has several facets, not all of which are easily seen at first glance. Mountain biking does have an inherent risk involved in merely climbing on a bike and riding it off-road. Yet the risk factor and the thrill of doing something risky safely, is what makes it attractive to many people. Consider physical risk, psychological risk (making someone so scared they will never get on a bike again) and emotional risk (is there so much peer pressure that not going off that jump may damage a rider's reputation or standing within a group?) when you are leading a group of riders. Ultimately what you need to do is make a judgement in weighing up the benefits of doing something risky, with the risks of injury (physical, psychological or emotional) associated with doing that risky thing. That is what risk management is all about. After all, if we wanted to avoid the risk of injury when mountain biking, the easiest way to achieve this would be to stay at home and not go mountain biking!

The risk benefit analysis (to give it a formal term) is something that happens in several phases and ways, all of which are linked and depend on one another. Firstly you need to consider the risks of your planned route or activity before you even go out the door. This is what most people understand as 'filling in a risk assessment' which they may have to do for work or other activity. But the process doesn't stop there as some believe it does. You'll need to visit the venue at least once so that you can be sure your form filling is accurate. Even then filling in the form is not enough - although that form filling should have been based around a careful consideration of the benefits of doing the activity and the risks of doing the activity. The next phase is a more immediate, on the day, process of risk benefit analysis, that you do when you arrive at the venue or meet the group, and may be influenced by such things as the weather, the ability of the group, or even how busy the trail is. Finally there is the ongoing, minute-by-minute risk benefit analysis that is truly dynamic in its form. You make decisions based on your experience, training and perhaps guidance from others. This professional judgement and decision making (as it is called in the terminology of the adventure sports coach) is some-

Through the ford, Elan Valley, Wales

thing that is little understood as to how it can be developed, save that it takes time to develop and involves gaining a wide range of experience.

The basics

As this book is intended to introduce riders to the concepts of leading and support those who may be aiming to gain a qualification, the list below sets out what I consider the minimum I would expect of a leader if I were assessing them for a leadership award. The list is not in a hierarchical order, but could be used as a valuable tick list in checking to make sure you've done all the things you need to before (and to some extent during) a ride or mountain bike session that you are leading, either by definition or nominally as you are the more experienced rider in a group.

Preparation and planning

If at all possible ride the route beforehand so you know what awaits you, where you can gather the group, and any specific hazards or features you will use to develop specific skills. Check access and environmental considerations, and if you're going out on a natural trail, prepare a route card. Plan emergency routes to help and identify where emergency services could access you at each stage of your route. Consider leaving a copy of the route card with someone who can notify the emergency services if you have not returned buy a certain time (and tell them what time, and what exactly to do if you haven't returned.)

Meeting the group

Meet them in a safe place (not the car park) and give them a clear briefing of what you plan for the session and what they can expect from you. Ask if they have specific requirements or things they want to get from the session. Go through your safety instructions and any specific command words you may use (e.g. a shout of 'trail' for overtaking riders).

During the ride

Dynamically manage the hazards and risks in the light of the benefits these may also offer. Use appropriate opportunities for coaching/teaching on both a group and individual level. Ensure the well-being of your group and consider where you position yourself in the group for maximum effectiveness, which may be at the front, at the back or somewhere in-between depending on the ability of the group and circumstances.

Photo 1.2: A safe place without distractions is really important for your initial meeting of the group, and safety briefing

Manage the progress of the group around the route as appropriate - thinking about how to manage sections of technical difficulty, singletrack or specific features, along with a clear indication of stopping places and what to do if something goes wrong.

After the ride

Review the activity session with the group and get and give feedback from/to individuals. Check over bikes and riders, and ensure they have returned any equipment that you may have lent out, and return bikes to the hire shop if they have been hired. If you have left a copy of the route card or expected return time with someone, contact them and let them know you have returned safely.

Specific aspects of leadership

So having just set out what I expect a leader to do as a minimum in their session, the following sections offer some advice and suggestions for some areas of group management which have the potential to cause uncertainty with those developing their leadership skills. The sections are not definitive rules, but offer some thoughts as to where you might start developing your own methods to solve problems often encountered with leading groups of mountain bikers.

Sections of technical difficulty, singletrack or a specific feature/hazard

If you decide that a section needs to ridden in a more managed way than just everyone riding together at their own pace, then there are several options available to you. This more often applies to downhill sections as gravity acting in the favour of the riders means there is less general control by each individual, but these principles can be applied to tight, technical singletrack climbs as well.

The easiest way is to tell your riders to keep a certain spacing between them. This could be a number of bike lengths, or a time delay (e.g. 'count to 10 before setting off after the rider in front'). Groups may need reminding of this, or you may change the spacing dependent on the terrain. The steeper the terrain, particularly downhill, the wider the spacing should be. Brief the group on what to do if they have to stop for whatever reason - do they get off the trail as quickly as possible, or do they signal in some way for the whole group to stop?

If you deem the section or feature, or your group, needs to be more closely managed then you will need to consider sending them down a section one at a time and having someway of controlling this. You could choose to give a clear end point (that you know from your pre-ride) and then you stay at the start of the section and send the riders in your group off at intervals or when you can see or they signal they have got to the bottom. For longer sections where this is needed you will need some way of signalling between the start and end of a section - this could be as simple as a whistle with the first person down to the end who blows it every time another rider makes it safely down, or as advanced as hand held, walkie-talkie style radios. My preference is to be the first down a section like this (so I can make a specific and dynamic on the spot risk benefit analysis judgement) and to make sure the group stop where they need to. Then I signal back to the next rider with a whistle blast. Two blasts indicate that no one continues as there has been a problem on the section so I can make my way back up without fear of being mown down by another rider. If you're using radios you can give one to a 're-lease controller' at the start and give them a verbal signal when it is safe and appropriate for the next rider to come down, with them bringing up the rear. Of course if you can see the start from the end, you can wave or signal visually in this manner too.

When riding, applying the general adventure sports leadership principle of CLAP will help you think about and then operate in as safe a manner as possible. CLAP originates in the world of whitewater paddling* but the principles can be applied (with guidance) to mountain biking.

The principles of CLAP

C - communication - clearly communicate to your group what you want them to do, what they need to do and what to do if things go wrong. Once you're moving how will you communicate with your group? For specific sections will you use visual or verbal communication?

L - line of sight - a tricky one in mountain biking as for safety reasons you are unlikely to have sight of your whole group of riders at once. But the principle really is connected with knowing what your group

*Ferrero, F. (2006) *Whitewater safety and rescue*, Pesda Press is doing and hence what you need to be doing at any one time. Thus, if each rider in a group can see the rider in front of them and behind them, they can pass a signal, be it visual or verbal back through the group, so you do therefore have an effective 'line-of-sight' albeit indirectly.

A – assess risk - something you do pre-ride and dynamically during the activity, based on things such as group ability, fatigue levels, time of day, difficulty of section etc.

P – position of most usefulness - where can you be most effective? At the front, at the back, in the middle, by a specific hazard, at the meeting point, at a potential spot for losing the trail?

If at each point you consider leading in light of these four principles then you will be doing the basics right, and be able to ensure the group is a safe as they can be (dependent on the level of risk you have deemed acceptable), and you will be in the right place to deal with situations which nay arise in the most timely and effective manner.

Riding on the road

Let's face it this is a book about mountain bike leadership so it seems a little odd to have a section dealing with road riding. However, the reality is that if you are riding natural trails you may often have to connect bits of them with some short road sections. Make no mistake, riding on the road with a group is by far the most dangerous thing you will do as a leader - far more so than the actual mountain bike/off road riding you really want to be doing. The reason is simple: in the off road sections, you have far more control over managing the risks, but on the road the main hazard (traffic) is completely outside your control.

The first thing to say about road riding is that the most important thing you can do to avoid accidents with motor vehicles is to be seen, no matter what time of day you are riding at. To do this, the minimum precaution I would use is a high-vis vest on the lead and last rider in a group. If you can give every rider a high-vis vest for the road sections, all the better. It

Photo 1.3: The disadvantage of riding as one big long single file snake: no safe stopping place, and oncoming traffic (albeit on a quiet rural road, Co. Wicklow, Ireland)

should go without saying that if you're riding at night, or dusk or dawn, each bike should have a white front light and red rear light also. Think about how you will arrange the group. Although it is possible to ride two abreast on the road, it is far more sensible and safer to stay in single file. However, you need to think about how vehicles will overtake your group. One long snake of riders is difficult for motorists to get past, so it is better to either ride in single file with several bike lengths between each rider (so a car can overtake one rider at a time and pull in between overtaking moves) or as small groups of two or three riders so vehicles can overtake in small batches. The decision as to the strategy to use is up to you based on how busy and wide the road is. On a quieter road a long snake of riders with appropriate spacing is fine, but on more busy roads, the smaller the groups and wider the spacing should be. Again, have clear stopping points where you can safely re-group and check on the group. Good communication between the groups and within a group can help keep everyone safe too. A shout of 'car up" (car behind, overtaking) or 'car down' (an oncoming car) can quickly pass the message to riders on quieter roads where they may have bunched or let their spacing close up as there is little traffic.

Road crossing with a group

The are two main aways to cross a road with a group of riders, and one also acts as a useful way to turn across traffic (turning right from a T junction for instance). Even if you are not intending to ride on a road, there are a number or trail centres that have main roads crossing them and so these need to be negotiated as part of leading a group there (for example the Follow the Dog route on Cannock Chase in the West Midlands).

The filter crossing

Here riders cross the road one at a time, controlled by a leader who has made the crossing first. The leader crosses over and waits on the left of the road but directly opposite the crossing point or T junction. This way they have full sight of all oncoming traffic. The group either waits by the side of the road to cross, or on the left hand side of the road some way back from the T junction. As the leader signals (usually a wave will suffice) one rider moves across the road and waits further down from the leader, or at the nearest safe place, preferably off the road where possible. This continues until the whole group is across. It is a time consuming method, but is by far the safest as only one rider at a time is exposed to traffic danger.

The gated crossing

This relies on the leader having a competent second or helper with them, and is far quicker than the filter crossing as it gets the whole group across at once. Its disadvantage is that the whole group is presented to the traffic danger at one time and can get mixed/tangled up in one another as they cross the road leading to being in the danger area (road) for longer.

It works by all the riders lining up next to one another, facing the road they need to cross. The leader is at one end with the assistant leader or competent second at the other end. The leader and second agree when to step out into the road (when there is an appropriate sized gap). They move to the middle of the road and then when checking it is clear again, signal the whole group to cross at once. The other problem with this method is that as the gap in traffic needs to be longer than for one rider crossing, you can sometimes wait quite a while for a suitable gap. As a rule of thumb on busy roads a filter crossing is the quickest and safest option, but on less busy roads the gated crossing works best.

Stopping for a rest, Beddgelert forest, Wales

2. Coaching

The bunny hop, Gwydyr Forest, Snowdonia

One aspect of leadership which is sometimes ignored is that of coaching. Its all very well having a great day out with your group and enjoying some adventures together, but are there things you could do to help your group improve their techniques? Probably. Could you have used parts of the route to coach these skills? Probably. Do you know what these techniques are? Probably. Do you know how to get your riders to improve? Well that's what this chapter is all about.

Coaching
(and teaching)

As the chapter page has already hinted, this part of the book is about the sometimes mysterious aspect of leadership that is coaching. In fact, coaching and teaching are two different things, but they are often discussed together in the context of learning and honing various skills. Whilst it is entirely possible to lead a group on a ride without paying any attention to improving their riding ability, it really is a missed opportunity if you don't do something to develop the group's skills as you ride. This could be technical skill (learning to log hop, for instance), exploration skill (navigation and route choice) or an intra-personal skill (such as overcoming fear or gaining confidence).

It has only recently been recognised that adventure sports, such as mountain biking, have their own peculiar characteristics when it comes to teaching, learning and coaching, and as such a specific pedagogy, or approach to teaching and learning, is still developing. That said, there are other adventure sports that have well developed bodies of knowledge concerning coaching, some of which can be transferred to mountain biking.

A lot of the information in this chapter is based on my own experience in coaching mountain biking and teaching people how to coach and teach a range of sports, for various national governing body awards. There is also much from my work as a coach educator within the more formalised and written down ideas on coaching paddlesport. As such, this chapter follows principles set out by Bill Taylor and his work on the chapter entitled 'Coaching' in the BCU Coaching Handbook.

Firstly let's be specific as to the differences between coaching and teaching. There are several definitions out there, but for the purposes of this chapter, I will define teaching as giving someone new information to develop a specific skill, and coaching as the honing and perfecting of that skill, relying on the fact that the student already knows and understands how to perform a skill, but they are still developing their own ability to match this. Coaching and teaching clearly overlap, and many of the skills in mountain biking are progressive, requiring a foundation skill to be mastered before moving on to a more advanced skill.

Secondly, the coaching and teaching discussed here is in the context of a leader on a ride or journey, not a specific skills based session. Although this is a skill that can be developed, this book is about mountain bike leadership so doesn't cover long term athlete development.

So what does coaching entail? Well, coaching is a complex activity that requires careful thought. It is in itself a thinking activity, and along with teaching (in this context) it can be distilled down to three key areas of competency, described on the next page. The important thing is that

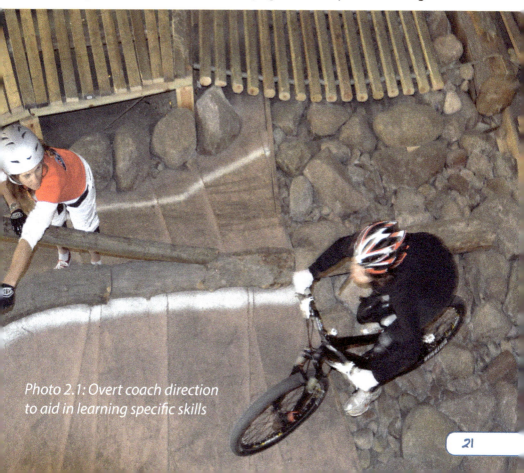

Photo 2.1: Overt coach direction to aid in learning specific skills

The Mountain Bike Leader's Handbook

coaching and teaching are not 'recipe style' skills where a method can be presented, and then anyone can apply this in any situation and get the same results. Rather the coach's role is more like that of the chef (to stick with the cooking analogy) who must take the ingredients and blend them to produce the final dish. The coach needs to blend their own skills and competencies in coaching and mountain biking to create the right fit for the clients/students they are working with.

Coaching competencies*

The skill of the coach relies on a complex interaction of the following competencies. Different coaches will have different strengths, which will change as they develop their own coaching ability. Below are the 3 main areas to consider in your development as a teacher and coach.

Knowledge

- About the subjects you are dealing with (hopefully this book will help develop some of these)
- About the group as individuals and their interactions with each other
- About the venue you've selected to deliver the session in

Decision making

- How you decide when and where to deliver your session - particularly in the context of a ride
- Deciding which methods/pedagogy/approaches are the best fit for your situation
- Decisions about the safety of the individuals and group as they interact with their often hazardous environment.

Actions

- Overt behaviours of the coach in their efforts to help students improve or learn a skill (photo 2.1)
- How the coach can actively manage the teaching part of the session to get the leaners on the right track.

*Adapted from an original by Taylor, B. (2006) Coaching in *Coaching Handbook*, Ferrero, F. (ed.) British Canoe Union/Pesda Press

As you develop your own competency in each of these areas, you become a better coach, but as already mentioned, coaching is a complex skill where small changes can have large impacts due to the interaction of factors not only the factors themselves.

Over time, as you lead more groups and hence practise your teaching and coaching skills, you will develop your own coaching philosophy. This is not a set of things you always do, more a set of guiding principles that often form subconsciously and underpin what you as a coach believe about the coaching process. You may not be able to write it down but your philosophy governs how, when and why you coach and teach. It is influenced by other people you work/ride with, coach education or leadership courses you do, things you read and other coaches who you observe in action. It is important to be aware of your own coaching philosophy, as just the same as leadership in general, you should play to your strengths as a coach. Usually the time you have coaching is relatively short as it may be at the start of the day to get the group competent to ride the route you've selected, or a short break in the journey to use a feature you've come across. My advice is to stick with what you know when in these situations to get the best fit between your coaching competencies and the needs of the group. If you try to adopt a different philosophy or approach you fairly quickly reduce your competency in at least one of the key areas noted opposite. If you want to try out a new approach, do it in a more familiar environment and one where there is less pressure - on a ride with friends, for instance.

The coaching process

If any coaching process is to be effective then there are a number of major themes that need to be considered by the leader/coach before they actually deliver the session. This could be as part of a pre-ride planning session, or it could be an on-the-fly type process as you come to a trail feature that lends itself to a particular skill, or you observe your group and deem it necessary to teach them a skill before they continue.

Planning - as I've previously said this can be long term planning (several days before the session) or short term/on-the-fly planning (judging how well the group are doing and thinking about how to give them more challenge whilst out on the ride).

Delivery or intervention - what are you actually going to do with the group? Set them a task or practice and intervene individually based on your observations? Teach a new skill by using a demonstration? The approach you take will be dependent your own technical ability and understanding, and also the approach and style of leadership you are using with your group at the time you introduce the coaching/teaching aspect of the ride.

Reasons - why are you coaching the group? Is it to add value to the ride or because they need a specific skill to complete the ride efficiently or enjoyably?

Participation incentive - how much will the group buy-in to what you are selling? Do they want to be coached/taught? Can they see the need for your coaching session? There is a great deal of difference in coaching riders who are out to actively improve and those who just want a good day out on a bike.

Details - how detailed do you need to be in your coaching? Sometimes this will depend on the reasons for the coaching, and the areas you have available. If you need a specific skill to complete a route, then choose a specific, detailed coaching/teaching activity. If you need to let riders develop along some general principles, then plan and deliver a session that takes a holistic view of the rider not the details of the movement.

Duration - how long will your intervention or session last? Is it something that needs a quick fix, or a skill that can be worked on throughout the ride, perhaps in some different contexts?

Each of these major themes interacts in a complex way and so must all be considered when looking into what makes a good coach and what allows them to deliver effective sessions. Effective sessions contain different elements and have at least a start, middle and end, although may have several of these as mini-'session-within-a-session' sections. When you start out, you need to address the issues of incentive/motivation and reasons early on so the group commits to following your instructions or taking part in the coaching activity you have planned. Equally you need to have some way of assessing their ability so you can tailor your session to the right level (where they will learn and not be bored) for each skill and specific feature. The middle of the session tends to have a task or practice focus and the end summarises what has been covered and perhaps looks to embed some learning via a review or plenary activity.

It's important to understand that the coaching process is often not a linear one, starting at point A and ending at point B. Rather, it often involves cycles, characterised very simplistically in the Plan/Do/Review model. There are mnemonics to help exemplify the coaching process, but I don't think they are always helpful as although they are represented as cyclic, they still move in one direction and are sequential. A better representation is seen in figure 2.2 which covers things that a leader may do when coaching and how they interact. It tries to illustrate that although there are complex interactions, the process is not haphazard and random, but has a focus. The things that a leader may do when they are coaching include:

- Observation and analysis
- Organising tasks and practice
- Questioning
- Giving feedback
- Demonstrating
- Giving verbal instructions and commands

An effective leader doing some effective coaching, will use some or all of these aspects, but how much of each and how they are linked depends on the skill of the coach in recognising what needs to be done.

The Mountain Bike Leader's Handbook

When you are coaching a group, remember that the focus should be on them as learners and not you as a skilful rider. The idea is that they improve their skills not just sit back and marvel at yours.

When you are planning any coaching, whether that is further ahead or on the fly, you need to consider the experience and ability of the group you are with, and if necessary how you will pitch the session or section

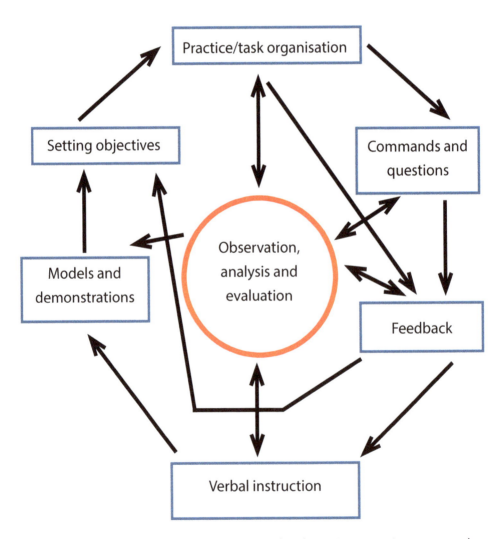

Figure 2.2 - coach behaviours in the direct intervention approach
(adapted from an original from Taylor, B. (2006))

of a ride at the right level for each of the riders. In teaching this is known as differentiation, and there is a degree of confidence as well as skill in delivering a session to a mixed ability group. Plan ahead and think how you can best use the feature or section of trail you will use to stretch the most able riders in your group, and also support those who need most help to develop their skills. Remember also in your planning that what your students *want* to do/learn is not always the same as what they *need* to learn. You need to try to satisfy both criteria even if they appear at first to be incompatible.

A useful tip is to actually write down the plan for the coaching part of your ride when you are first gaining experience as a leader or even as an experienced leader doing some coaching and teaching. Whilst this may seem like a lot of work, it really does make you think about whether you have covered each aspect described in figure 2.2 and how they will interact in your own delivery - which is something personal to you.

Your own coaching style will develop along with your philosophy over time. In the following sections we will look in a bit more detail at each of those coaching behaviours from figure 2.2 and the list earlier in the chapter to try to piece together the tools a leader can use to be an effective teacher and coach. As the diagram in figure 2.2 suggests the behaviours are not hierarchical and as such you should not pay any special attention to the order in which they appear. The general approach which has the coach playing an active role in the intervention and teaching/coaching process is known as a direct intervention approach, and the behaviours shown in figure 2.2 are characteristic of this type of approach.

Special note on learning styles and presentation

There has been much written about the learning styles, or preferences, of individuals, and quite a lot said about how learners can be classified as either Visual, Auditory or Kinaesthetic in the way they prefer to receive information and instruction. This has a direct impact on how the coach and teacher should deliver their sessions.

This learning style categorization (also sometimes known as VAK learning) comes from an extrapolation of the work of Howard Gardner on the different or multiple intelligences. Whilst still commonly thought to be a good way to coach, research in the late 2000's has shown that it is a very unhelpful and inaccurate way of thinking about how people learn. This has been seen as down to the fact that it is not what Gardner intended for his work and is based on extrapolations of the ideas not data or research findings. More recent research shows that not only is trying to categorise leaners as one type or another wrong, but that it can also be detrimental to a learner's perception on how they can learn, and so some avenues become closed to them as they associate themselves with a labelled 'learning style'. Far better, and in line with current understanding, is to allow all learners to access the information through a combination of each of the mechanisms discussed above (that is, visually - through demonstrations, audibly - through instruction and explanation, and kinaesthetically - through task based practice). Thus, as a coach if you are aware of these aspects and try to incorporate aspects of each into your session, you will be more effective in teaching your learners what they need to know, in the format that best suits them in that context and at that time.

Observation and analysis

Fundamental to the coaching process, is the process of observing your learners and analysing what you are seeing. It should be obvious that you need a good knowledge of the skill so that you can identify what is right and what is wrong with what the student is doing. It also helps in knowing the common errors people make with specific skills so you can home in on them and check specifically for these issues and fix them early on in the skill development. In order to help in this, chapter 5 contains a detailed description of common useful riding skills and also some of the common errors.

It is important that you as the coach have a clear picture in your mind of what the skill performed correctly looks like, so that you can make a comparison with what you see. Think about where you position yourself in relation to what you want to observe - can you see all that you need to? If not move to somewhere you can. Bear in mind that the position that is best for observing may not be the position which is best for giving feedback, so you may need to be mobile through the session.

When you're watching students perform a skill or complete a practice task, there are 3 main ways in which you can approach the act of observation.

Holistic - this is all about looking at the big picture and seeing what is going on overall. It relies upon you as the leader/coach having a clear picture of what you expect to see and directly comparing this with what is in front of you. This relies heavily on the coach's experience to recognise the overall skill being performed correctly. In mountain bike coaching, a top tip is to look at the body shape of the rider to use this holistic approach. If the body shape matches what you perceive as the correct shape then all well and good. If not, then you need to intervene.

Deductive - as you gain experience (and read chapter 5) you will begin to see that there are common errors made when learning or refining a particular skill (for instance riders who try to pull up with their arms for the log hop instead of springing up using their legs). Look for these small or common errors specifically when you are observing and if you spot them you know what can be done to give fairly quick results in overcoming the problem.

Analytical - this relies on specific markers you are looking for. In a mountain biking content the biggest one as already mentioned is body shape, but also you need to look at speed, gear, braking, feet and head. If you analyse each of these components, you will find one or more of them are not in line with the image you have of a successful skill demonstration or task completion. Once you have focussed on that specific issue, you can pull back and analyse another area, or use a more holistic approach from then on.

Once you have observed your learners performing a task, it is important to then analyse what they have done, in order to know how to respond. Take your time in analysing - don't rush it and if that means you don't give feedback straight away because you are reflecting on and analysing what you have seen, this is no bad thing. Sometimes learners need to have a chance for a bit of trial and error before you say anything. Research generally shows that skills learnt through trial and error (with some guidance) are more securely embedded than if the coach tells the learner 'the answer' early in a session.

Some aspects of a rider's demonstrating may be obvious but have little effect on the actual move being learned. Be clear in your mind if you are identifying a symptom or a root cause. Addressing symptoms has short term impact - look for the root cause for longer term results. This identification and differentiation in your mind comes with experience and a secure knowledge of the actual skill and how its component parts link together, as well as an image of the overall view of the skill.

Sometimes you may not be able to see the causes of the problem, and this is where questioning comes in to try to collect more information for your analysis process. Try using open questions, but be specific about the information you want from the rider to help you in your analysis.

Towards the end of your analysis process (that may be all of a few minutes or a longer period), ask yourself whether the learner actually needs you to pass a comment on what just happened? If they are practising the log hop and are progressing well but then have one try where the front wheel stays on the ground, do they really need you to acknowledge this, or do they already know? Being told the obvious is frustrating and can mean learners lose focus in being unhappy or cross with themselves, and no one likes taking criticism when they know they've done something wrong. The other thing to think about is whether you have time in the short coaching section of a day's ride to actually fix and work on this particular issue. If not, then it may be as well to leave the issue and work on things that can be sorted in the time you have available.

Organising tasks and practice

When it comes to setting a task to practise or work on a specific technique, there are two approaches that you can take. They are what is known as blocked practice and random practice. They each have their advantages and disadvantages and uses, although research evidence suggests that random practice is better at ensuring a competence in a skill is embedded and securely learnt. Blocked practice tends to give rapid results but there is not the persistence in the improvements made; next time out they are forgotten or need further work as they are not embedded.

Blocked practice involves riders doing the same exercise or task over and over again with feedback at appropriate times from the leader. Random practice involves different skills being practised one after the other. In a mountain biking context and example of blocked practice would be placing a small stick or branch across the track and getting riders to (in turn) try and log hop or bunnyhop the stick. This has the advantage of allowing the coach to manage the group and observe/give feedback whilst ensuring group safety, and all the group are working towards the same goal. Random practice might be riders travelling around a circuit, such as a skills track where there are a number of obstacles that they need to deal with in sequence, such as rollers, berms, a drop off and board walk. The coach needs to choose what feedback they give to each rider, and it can be differentiated by obstacle, skill or ability.

Questioning

Questioning has several uses for the coach, not least in checking the understanding of the student. This can be at a basic level of understanding what they have been asked to do, or at a deeper a level of understanding what is required to affect a change in their performance. In this context, closed questions, (that is ones with short answers such as yes or no) are really useful. If you need more detail then you can ask a student to repeat back in their own words what you have just said to them, and ask them what this means for what they have to do next.

Open questions (those that require some thought or processing by the student) are really useful in a true coaching (as opposed to teaching) situation. Skilful questioning can draw out of students what they have done, what they are doing and what they need to do to improve. Of course, questioning can't draw out what someone doesn't know, which is why it is important to teach new skills and not try to get learners to discover them. This guided discovery approach is time consuming in the context of a ride with coaching/teaching sessions built in to the journey, and has also been criticised by research that suggests the knowledge constructed during discovery has no guarantee of being correct and is incredibly difficult to unpick if it is wrong. My advice in the context of mountain bike leadership is to teach new skills and coach students once you have taught them the principles and movements required for a particular skill. The timing of questioning is also important. If you want someone to answer a question about what they are doing, either give them time to reflect and digest what has happened so that they can answer your question, or prime them before they perform a task so they know what they are looking for in order to answer your question.

Generally open questions are good to use when you are developing an idea or concept where there are clear links to prior knowledge, but closed questions allow you to direct a learner's attention in a particular direction. Bear in mind that whilst a degree of open questioning on feedback, or to try to draw out intrinsic feedback from learners is useful, it can be very frustrating for a student who wants 'an answer' or direct feedback from a coach who refuses to give it by only asking questions. If you do use questioning, make sure you listen carefully to the answers and then act on, or take on board the answers given. Failure to do so will mean you miss a valuable tool in your analysis, and dilutes the authenticity of your leadership (see chapter 1).

Feedback

Feedback is the information that goes back to a learner, upon which they base their next decisions and movements. It can come in two distinct forms: external and internal. External feedback, also called extrinsic feedback comes from outside the student. This maybe in the form of a verbal message from the coach/teacher, but can equally be a nonverbal gesture or motion by the coach. Internal or intrinsic feedback is that which the learner feels from inside their own body and mind.

Both types of feedback are useful when coaching a session, but need a little more explanation so that they can be used effectively in a mountain biking context.

Firstly let's look at intrinsic feedback as it is much misunderstood and hence under utilised. As a rider performs a skill or move, they will gather information from their senses as to what they feel they are doing. This may be as simple as feeling the force of impact through the legs when landing from a drop off, or more subtle in feeling off-balance when riding a narrow path. As a coach you can tap into this intrinsic information, providing you know what it should feel like when things are working correctly, and can put this into a verbal form to communicate it clearly to the riders. Try to stick to feelings and things that can be clearly identified as a result of the skill. Stay away from the more ethereal concepts such as flow, and stick to forces, balance, and effort. A useful approach I often use is to allocate a numerical scale to a feeling and once you have got the students to understand the scale and feeling, they have an internal measure of what they should do, and importantly whether they actually followed your instructions after performing a skill. An example may be the amount of effort they put into pedalling, where 1 is very little, almost coasting along, and 5 is a flat out stand on the pedals sprint. If I'm getting someone to try a technical uphill section I'll then ask them to ride the section at about a 4 on this scale and see how it goes. This gives them an idea of what it should feel like to ride the section. Their intrinsic feedback then tells them if they were over doing it (indicating some other aspect of their technique needs work) or under doing it (and perhaps it was harder than they expected). Another obvious example is in landing drop offs. In coaching this, I ask the riders to imagine they have a scale on their legs where total compression and knees bent as far as possible is a 5 and standing totally straight up is a 1. As we progress I can describe what they should feel as they land the corresponding height of drop off.

Beware that intrinsic feedback can only go so far though. Its major disadvantage is that it is subjective and if you haven't quite got the student to understand what the feeling is, they will not understand the feedback mechanism you are trying to get them to use. Thus, intrinsic feedback is useful with learners whom you know slightly better or have spent more time with, so you can gauge their understanding of your ideas and requests better. It is really useful for advanced riders who need to polish and hone skills and want to be more coach-independent, but you always need to use it with other forms of feedback that you have more direct control over.

Extrinsic feedback can come from the coach or the environment. The environment feedback can be in terms of the student understanding how they have performed a skill in relation to 'markers' you have identified in the surrounding area. An example, and one I often use with novices when teaching them to brake smoothly, is to draw two parallel lines in the dust/dirt/gravel of the trail. The first mark is where they start to brake, the second line is where they should have stopped by, and for those who need a bit more, also without skidding. Thus they can gain feedback from the environment, to know whether they have achieved the objective of stopping, whilst under control.

Extrinsic feedback from the coach can be verbal or nonverbal, although there is a tendency for less experienced leaders to use only the verbal method. Sometimes a quick thumbs up or a wave can provide all the feedback a rider needs. Often, however the coach needs to use verbal feedback to convey a slightly more complex idea. It's important to remember to praise effort where needed, but don't confuse that with success at the task, otherwise someone trying hard but getting the skill wrong thinks that they're doing ok. It's important to be specific with what your are giving feedback on as much as it is important to individualise that feedback. When giving verbal feedback, operate on the principle that less is more. The less verbal information you give to the student the more likely they are to turn that specific bit of feedback into an action. Think about what you are going to say before you say it. Let the student give their own feedback if they chose to first, and then give your view. You will learn a lot about their perceptions of their own ability to perform a skill and how they felt it went (intrinsic feedback) by listening to what they say to you. Don't be so intent on giving your pearl of wisdom that you ignore their thoughts.

In order to make feedback effective think about these three things when you want to give a student feedback:

- Rehearse in your mind what you want to say, then, when you're ready, get the learner's attention
- Wait for the learner to finish the task or activity before trying to give feedback
- Only give the feedback when they are ready (you'll know this from their body language and expression as well as them usually moving towards you to better hear what you have to say).

When giving feedback, try to use the following framework.

- Give a specific example of the action/activity you are giving feedback about e.g. 'On that last attempt at the log hop, you really exploded up from the bike'
- Describe the effect that you saw e.g. 'That's why the front of the bike lifted so high - it was at least 20cm from the ground'
- Give instructions as to the changes that need to be made e.g. ' This time try exploding upwards a little later, closer to the log, so the front wheel clears it. Can you do that? Great, off you go', or get the student to repeat the task again to embed the learning.

The Mountain Bike Leader's Handbook

When giving feedback you need to think about where you position yourself to be most effective in that process. Do you want to be at the end of the task to give instant reflection or at the start of a task to allow the leaner some time before they get to you for some internal reflection on their performance. Try to keep it brief - only one point to work on if possible. This means you need to identify (from your observations) the change that will have the greatest impact on the performance of the skill. Make sure you allow the learner time to process their intrinsic feedback (even if you've not set anything specific to look for). This takes about 10 seconds in most people. Once you've given your brief feedback, get the learner back on the task - your feedback will be most effective if they can practise the skill again within a minute. This takes some organising if you have a line of people waiting to ride a feature, so think about having concurrent activities that can work on the same skill so that your group are continuously occupied without too much waiting around. Think about how you can check that both you and the student are thinking and talking about the same incident. Don't be afraid to criticise a particular movement, as long as you follow it up straight away with a description or demo of the correct movement.

Finally in this section on feedback, an important reminder: as the leader, teacher and coach of a group, don't forget to listen to and act on the feedback you get from the group - especially if that feedback is that they are bored/tired/cold or just want to get on with the ride!

Demonstrating

Demonstrations of a certain skill are a very common and often effective way of modelling a particular skill. However, poor demonstrations can be counter productive and give learners the wrong idea. Even if you give the correct explanation after giving an erroneous demo, your students will more than likely remember and refer to the mental image they have captured of the demo not the words of the explanation.

Whilst many skills require some technical movement of the bike or its controls, I'd strongly recommend that when demonstrating mountain bike skills you get the group to focus on the body shape of the rider as this is the most important aspect of most skills. If the body shape matches a good demo, then the other more subtle aspects of the skill can be tweaked with targeted feedback. In chapter 5 on riding skills, I have highlighted the body shapes and movements associated with each skill, and I would encourage you to adopt this approach when coaching or teaching a skill.

Below are a few top tips for giving or using effective demonstrations - remember that it doesn't have to be you who does the demo, and sometimes you can use a group member to great effect to boost their confidence and self-esteem by having them demo for you.

- Make sure all the group can see the demo
- Make sure any other markers you are using (such as a gate or landmark to begin a specific motion) are also in sight.
- The demo needs to be easily copied by the group (so you need to take into account where they are at in their learning at that moment)
- Do the demo in silence - allow the group to concentrate on one source of input at once. This is harder if you are not doing the demo as there is usually a desire to give a commentary on the demo.
- Do the demo in real time, not slow motion. Usually riders need to see the whole skill as it looks when they will do it - perhaps later when you want to break down specific aspects for certain individuals you can do slowed versions, but generally these aren't that helpful.
- Try and avoid negative demos - steer clear of the 'don't do it like this' demo, or the one where the demonstrator does the wrong thing (a risk when using someone other than you to demo, or if you can't actually do the skill you're teaching). No demo at all is better than a negative one.
- Give the leaners key points to watch for - perhaps what is the overall body shape, how do the rider's arms look at this point etc.

- Tell your group when the demo is starting and finishing so they know when to pay close attention.
- Use others to demonstrate (where appropriate). As already stated this is good if you can't do the skill well, but it is also helpful as it makes the skill seem achievable by someone with less experience than you (particularly good when working with novice groups).
- Give the group a chance to practice what they have seen, fairly soon after the demo. Don't stand talking after the demo, let them get on and practice.

Giving verbal instructions and commands

Verbal instructions and commands are those bits of information that you need to communicate to the students in a direct and succinct manner. It's not quite the same as feedback as these may have no direct observational basis. Clear and timely verbal communication is vital to getting the learners to understand what you want them to do, and sometimes why they need to do it. Always try to be as clear as you can, and plan what you are going to say before you say it. Every detail of what a coach says is taken in by the students and if there is more than one way of interpreting it then there is a risk that someone will get the wrong idea! Make your instructions specific to the task or situation that the student is in, and relate your instructions to that context. Think about timing - most people can't take on board verbal instructions as they are performing a physical task. Thus, wait until the activity has stopped or the specific practice task has been completed. Try to position yourself so that there are no distractions behind/around you to draw attention away from what you are saying. Work on the principle that less is more - in other words the less you say, the more able the learner is to be able to process what you have said and turn this into a physical action. Once things get complicated the learner's energy and brain power goes into deciphering what you meant and their body goes back to doing what is knows best or has always done. If you want change, choose your words carefully and keep them to an absolute minimum. This is especially true of less experienced riders. It is also important to check that the instructions have been received and understood. There are different methods for doing this - a simple 'do you understand?' or 'do you get that?' can do it, but sometimes it is helpful to get the student to repeat or summarise what you have just said back to you so you know that it has gone in. Finally, once you have given and instruction, allow time for the learner to actually do what you've asked before giving any feedback or further instruction. This time period will be different for each learner, but generally coaches and teachers don't wait long enough and continuously bombard the student with information and instruction, so the value of each nugget of information is drastically reduced.

Some random practice on the pump track

3. Environmental Impact

One of the key responsibilities of a leader discussed in chapter 1 is to ensure a sustainable approach to the environment in which they operate. In order to do this it is important to understand the impact that mountain biking, and particularly groups of mountain bikers have on the environment - be that out in the wild or at the trail centre.

Uncle Fester, Coed y Brenin

Uncle Fester

DRAGON'S BACK

BEAST

CYFLYM COCH

The Mountain Bike Leader's Handbook

Environmental Impact
Being a sustainably literate leader

One of the key responsibilities of leading a group of mountain bikers is to consider, and where possible, minimise the impact you and your group have on the environment. Why is this important? Partly to preserve the natural environment so that it can be used by others or yourself in future, and partly because if you don't, the reputation and hence access rights we as mountain bikers currently enjoy will be reduced. This even applies to some degree to the man made trails at purpose built centres, and this chapter sets out to consider some things to think about when planning your mountain bike session/route, and also how to be a more sustainably literate leader. Of course, all of these points can apply to you as an individual rider, but their importance is amplified when you are responsible for larger groups who potentially may use the same area more often.

Generally mountain bikers get a bad press for damaging the environment and as leaders there is also an inherent responsibilty in taking more than just ourselves on trails which may be damaged as a result of our passage. There is now some research from the US and Australia[*] that shows that actually mountain bikers are no more damaging in terms of path erosion than walkers, although the research does find that both do more damage in the wet than in dry conditions. However, be warned that these findings are not well known and there is still a general perception of the mountain biker ripping up the trail/turf/track as they zoom past with no care for their impact at all.

Path/trail erosion

This is probably the most obvious and perhaps contentious impact, not least because it is often very obvious. Riding leaves tyre marks and the more knobbly the tyres and softer the ground, the bigger and deeper the marks. We cannot eliminate this from our riding, but riding with consider-

[*]Darlow, J. (2015) Research reveals walkers do more damage to trails than mountain bikers, *Mountain Bike Rider*, November 2015

ation of where the actual path/trail lies is key. Try to stay on the marked/worn trail where you can, and avoid making detours that end up making the path wider. This also applies to cutting corners at trail centres, as there are many examples of riders who don't seem to appreciate that the curves of a trail aid its flow, or that the hairpins turns in a switch back are there to make the riding easier than going straight up the hill. If there are sections of trail covered in boardwalk, it should be obvious to use the wooden way as it likely crosses delicate or just plain unrideable ground. If you're going to session a section, pay attention to how your group will make their way back to the start of the feature you are using. Ideally this would be back along the track they have ridden, not pushing up alongside, cutting a new path next to the existing trail. Look at the feature you are aiming to use and assess how suitable it is for what you want to do. A small drop off with a muddy landing is fine for a couple of riders to go over in the course of their route, but a group of 8 riders repeatedly riding over and dropping down from it will have a very marked effect on the downside of the drop. Of particular importance when trying to minimise erosion, is some good teaching and coaching on braking. As well as being key to riding smoothly and with flow, good, controlled and planned braking is also important in reducing the erosive effect of mountain bikes as they pass over a section of trail. Skids, whilst looking cool for a while, damage both the tread on the tyre and the ground underneath it in that they deliberately cause the tyre to slide and hence grab and move whatever is underneath it at

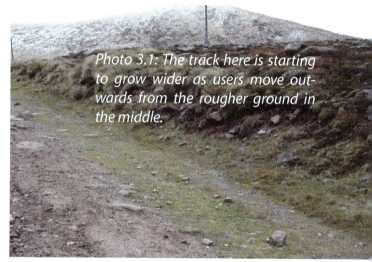

Photo 3.1: The track here is starting to grow wider as users move outwards from the rougher ground in the middle.

the time, be that turf, gravel or moss. In short, don't skid! The other issue caused by reactive and sudden braking, is braking bumps. These are particularly common at trail centres and if not repaired regularly they can present a hazard to other riders. They are caused by heavy braking near a turn, bend or other feature where riders need to slow down. As the brakes are applied, the weight of the rider moves forward as their body continues to move forward while the bike slows underneath them. As the weight moves forward, the fork compresses, but there is still an increased pressure on the front wheel, causing an uneven compacting of the trail beneath. As the weight of the rider moves back and compresses the rear end there is a compression from the back wheel (on full-sus bikes this is similar yet slightly less forceful). Many riders doing this in the same place causes small indentations to appear as the trail is compressed. This small bump formation then makes the trail more bumpy and less grippy so more riders brake harder because of the braking bumps which in turn makes them deeper and the cycle continues until either the depressions are filled in or the bumps

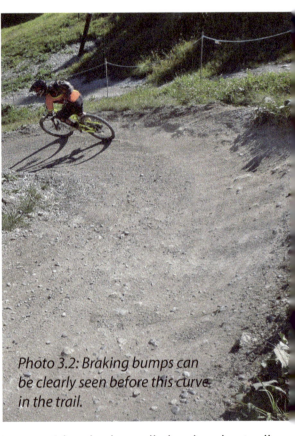

Photo 3.2: Braking bumps can be clearly seen before this curve in the trail.

are smoothed off. At the extreme, riders brake really hard and actually skid into the corners, causing the wheels to lock and literally bounce over the trail, causing deeper and slightly more spread out bumps to form, which then add to the difficulty of riding the corner smoothly. Modern trail centres tend to build berms into the trails for turns to avoid the need for this sudden braking, or line corners with harder, more compacted rock and stone which is less compressible. Teaching your group to brake progressively and in a planned way before they get to a corner will allow them to minimise the contribution they make to braking bumps, and ride the corner/turn carrying more speed and hence make the turn smoother.

Photo 3.3: Berms are often built at corners on man-made routes to help carry speed through the corner and avoid the creation of braking bumps.

The final point to consider is where you congregate or gather your group, either for a coaching briefing, to inform them of the nature of the next section, or to await other riders and keep the group together. This will commonly be at the end of a technical/downhill section, or just after a larger feature. Be aware of the potential erosive effect a group can have even just waiting around for a short period on a narrow trail. If and when you are able to ride the trail before you bring your group it is worth planning the points where you will stop so as to minimise the erosive impact and also to ensure the safety of the group. Good practice at trail centres is to try to meet on the fire roads/wide tracks which intersperse most trail centre sections as they are already wider and usually surfaced with a harder to erode material.

Litter

Whilst not only relating to mountain biking groups, there are some specific things to be aware of when leading mountain bike groups. The most obvious thing in regards to litter is that if you brought it with you, take it home. Pay particular attention to this when you get your group together as it is at stopping points where riders may pull out a chocolate bar or energy gel sachet to keep them going and not think about what they do with the rubbish afterwards.

Other litter commonly seen at trail centres are punctured inner tubes and the boxes from the new ones installed, left by the side of the trail, along with snipped cable ties where people have made some trail side repairs and forgotten to clear up after themselves. In addition, riders sometimes leave rather more valuable items behind, such as goggles, tools, pumps and even jackets.

Thinking of some things as 'biodegradable' is also quite unhelpful. Orange and banana peel, which technically being natural material that will break down in the environment, will take a long time to do so, and need to go in the bin and not on the trail. Cardboard packaging, again whilst being biodegradable as a material, often contains plastic coatings, and inks that are not, so should be removed to a proper recycling/rubbish point. A particular bugbear of mine is plastic energy drink bottles which seem to cover the ground at trail widening points or the tops of long climbs.

Noise

A group of riders creates considerable noise when moving along a trail, let alone when they are enjoying themselves and 'whooping' as they go. Whilst no one expects a group to ride in silence, you need to give consideration to what you may be disturbing with your noise. On open moorland, there are may ground nesting birds that may be disturbed by your noise, or in woodland you may disturb the small mammals that inhabit the ground and trees themselves. If you are on a natural trail you need to also be considerate of other users of the countryside - not that they have any more right than you to enjoy the natural environment, but that your use of the area shouldn't overly detract from theirs. Thus as well as riding considerately or allowing walkers to pass or get out of the way with appropriate warnings, try to be quieter around other track users. This particularly applies to horse riders - as with driving, horses can be easily unsettled by a noisy, often brightly coloured rider coming past quickly, or squealing brakes. Multiply this by the number of people in your group and it can be quite unsettling for both horse and rider. Ride considerately when you encounter horse riders, perhaps even thinking about getting off or stopping until they have passed.

Access restrictions

There are sometimes temporary restrictions placed on access to certain parts of a trail centre or natural trails for environmental reasons. If this is the case it is important that you respect these restrictions, and part of your planning process will be to find out what if any restrictions are in place before you take a group to an area. The following chapter contains more information on access issues, but if you are unsure, then a good source of information is usually the local bike shop (LBS), or local riders' forum on the web.

Plant life

By riding on trails and not widening them you can minimise the impact you have on plant life. However, be aware of special areas of conservation on your route, or rare/delicate plants and fungi that grow right next to the trail and can be damaged by an ill placed foot or bike tyre when resting or waiting for other group members. Again the LBS or a ride around the route yourself before you take a group will help in identifying where these areas are, and how you can minimise the impact you have on them.

Photo 3.4: A toadstool growing within inches of the Beast trail, Coed y Brenin

4. Access

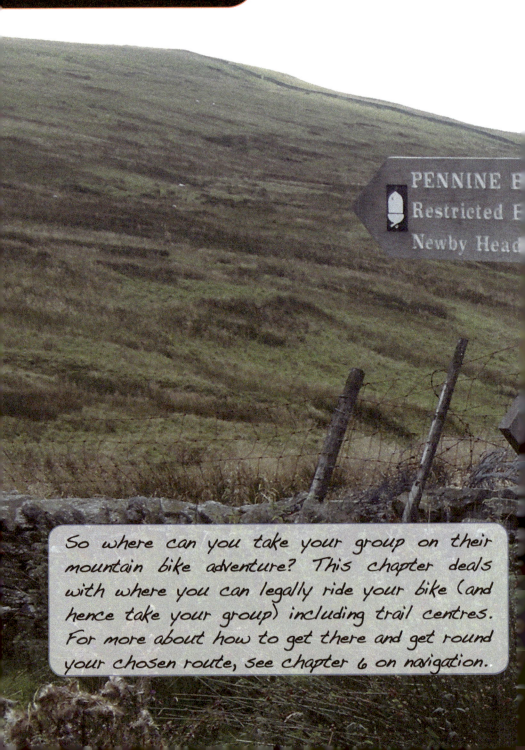

So where can you take your group on their mountain bike adventure? This chapter deals with where you can legally ride your bike (and hence take your group) including trail centres. For more about how to get there and get round your chosen route, see chapter 6 on navigation.

Cross roads, Pennine Bridleway

Access
(Where you can go)

When you plan your ride for your group, whatever your aims, you need to know that you can legally ride where you want to go. The short answer to "Where can you ride?" is anywhere, as long as you have the permission of the landowner. However, in practice most of us don't know or can't find out who the land owner is, so we have to use rights of way, which are just that; paths, tracks and trails across private land where we have a right to access. Another consideration as to where to ride your bike is where *should* you ride. This is perhaps better dealt with in chapter 3 on the environmental impact of mountain biking with groups. This section specifically refers to access issues in the UK - for other areas check out the web, or the best source for local knowledge, the local bike shop (LBS).

Rights of way

The easiest way to check if there is a right of way where you want to go is to use a map. Ordnance Survey maps cover the whole country at 1:25000 scale and 1:50000 scale and other companies such as Harvey Maps produce maps at 1:10000, 1:25000 and 1:40000 to certain popular areas of the country. Most maps will mark on them where public rights of way go, but there are different types of rights of way, and according to their designation you can either walk, ride or sometimes drive along them.

As mountain bikers we need to know where we can and can't ride our bikes. That is not to say you can't travel on all public rights of way with our bikes, but you can only *ride* on certain types of right of way. From time to time the designation of rights of way does change so its worth checking with local guides, bike shops or the local council as to whether a right of way has changed either designation or its position.

Of course you can ride you bike on the road (not the pavement) in most places, and specific road riding and group management techniques are covered in chapter 1.

There are also a myriad of paths and tracks across the British Isles which have been used for centuries, but to which no legal right exists. Again local knowledge is key here, and local guides or the local bike shop are well worth talking to.

Since public access to open country was enshrined in law in the Countryside and Rights of Way Act (2000) - CROW- things have got a lot better, legally, for those of us choosing to head out of town into open country. However, the CROW does not give us the right to walk or ride wherever we choose. Whilst modern maps show designated "access land" there may be seasonal restrictions and/or agreed access points (usually marked on maps).

Of the many types of rights of way the two most common are public footpaths, and public bridleways. Wading through all the legal speak, and unless there are specific local by-laws, you may not ride your bike on a public footpath (although you can walk along pushing it), and you may ride on public bridleway. There are also permissive footpaths and bridleways marked on most maps where the landowner has agreed for a period to allow public access. These are usually marked in a different colour to public rights of way.

There are a couple of other public rights of way you may ride on - restricted byways, and byways open to all traffic (referred to as BOATs and open to motorised vehicles such as 4x4 and motocross/quad bikes). There was a former designation which is still seen on some older maps, a road used as a public path (RUPP) which you may also ride on.

So, you can ride on most rights of way (except public or permissive footpaths), where you have permission from the landowner (for instance the Forestry commission give permission by marking and even building specific mountain bike routes on their land), or on public roads (not the pavement).

Please note that this is the situation for England, Wales and Northern

Ireland. The situation in Scotland is different in that a public right of way is any path which connects two public places, and has been open for people to walk on for at least 20 years. However, local councils are not required to mark or sign rights of way. Under the Land Reform Act (Scotland) (2003) rights of way exist to include access for mountain bikers. This in practice is fine on hard surfaces, but care should be taken on singletrack/soft ground, not least for the safety of other users and more pertinently for environmental reasons.

More information on access in Scotland can be found on the web by searching for "Scottish Outdoor Access Code".

Other than legal rights of way and environmental considerations, access may also be restricted by the time of year, for instance due to shooting, hunting, military operations (such as artillery or ground exercises), controlled burning, tree felling, harvesting or wildlife concerns such as nesting birds. If you are travelling in a national park the relevant office will have information on these seasonal restrictions, or the local wildlife trust should be able to advise. Outside these then the local bike shop or the web should provide up to date information.

The legal rights of way for a popular route in the Peak district can be seen in figure 4.1. A BOAT runs South West to North East across Houndkirk Moor (centre of the page), there are numerous footpaths to the west, (left) running roughly North to South along the Burbage valley from Burbage Bridge, and in the South East corner of the map can be seen the bridleways running through the Blacka plantation.

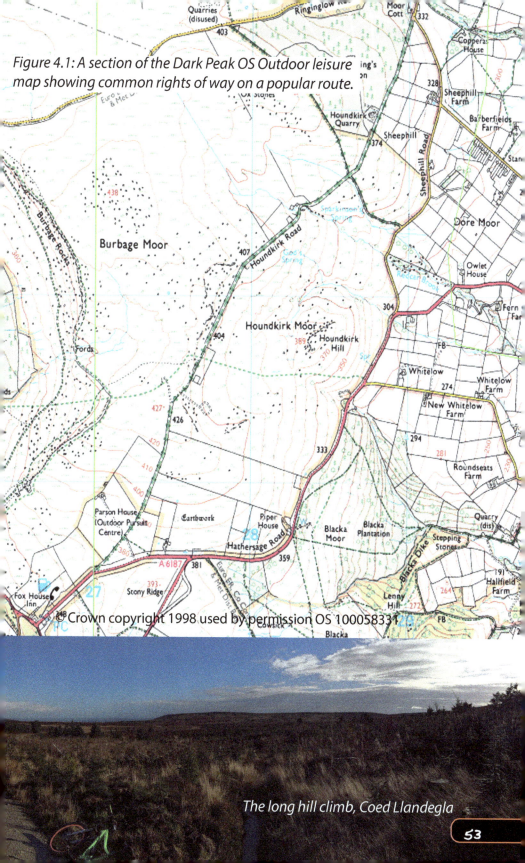

Figure 4.1: A section of the Dark Peak OS Outdoor leisure map showing common rights of way on a popular route.

The long hill climb, Coed Llandegla

The Mountain Bike Leader's Handbook

Trail centres

Trail centres represent a really useful facility to the mountain bike leader. They have their variations, but many will have a cafe, toilets and bike hire establishment on site, and with waymarked trails, offer a wide variety of riding for all abilities. Of course, you still need to choose your trail to match the ability of the group, but this is made easier by the generally accepted colour coding of routes according to difficulty.

Green routes are the easiest, consisting mainly of fire roads and hard packed tracks - they are suitable for families, younger children or those who need to build confidence on a bike. They tend to be of a shorter length so can be completed quickly - perhaps as a warm up or as a way of assessing a group's ability.

Blue routes introduce some sections of singletrack and require an ability to handle a bike on both up and downhill sections over slightly rougher ground than a green route. They may have some easier technical features such as rollers, gentle berms or switchbacks and very small drop-offs. A relatively fit group with a little coaching at the start should be able to handle a blue route.

Red routes mark the boundary between the 'most people can ride this' and the 'technical skill required' type trails. On red routes you can expect technical features such as berms, doubles, tabletops, small drop-offs and off-camber sections. A red route would not be suitable for a novice group as their first ride, but would be a great place to develop and hone skills. They are also likely to have features that can be sessioned in isolation if you are looking to coach a specific riding skill.

Black routes are technical trails that can be *a little* harder than a red route or *a whole lot* harder. They usually require a higher level of commitment as well as technical skill and may be significant in length or exposure, adding to the seriousness of the trail. On black routes you can expect to find steep downhill sections, technical climbs, large drop-offs/

rock steps, cut-outs, and boulder gardens.

Some trail centres also have skills/jumps parks or pump tracks to further hone skills - which are sometimes also graded, but this is not so universal so worth checking with the centre you're visiting. Significant hazards such as large drop-offs also tend to have prominent hazard notices as well to give warnings.

When using a trail centre, you need to be aware of other users, as you'll almost certainly encounter more riders there than out on a natural trail. General consideration and common sense should guide you, but there are a few specifics worth mentioning so as to make your time at a trail centre both useful and enjoyable.

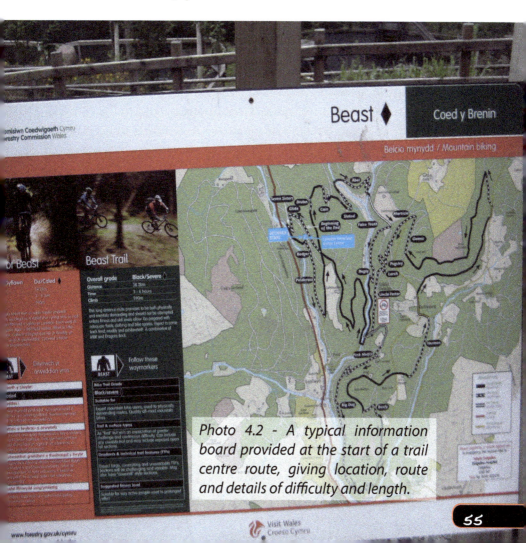

Photo 4.2 - A typical information board provided at the start of a trail centre route, giving location, route and details of difficulty and length.

Meeting/briefing

Gather your group in a safe and sensible place - the middle of the car park is not ideal as you will pose a hazard to traffic and your group. The start of the trail you intend to ride is also not a great place to group together as you will not doubt be blocking the way of other users and riders. So, ideally somewhere a little bit out of the way -ideally at the skills or warm up area.

Checking the bikes over

Always get your group (and keep and eye on them whilst they're doing it) to check over their bikes. If they're hired bikes you have the opportunity of spotting potential mechanical problems before you get far from the centre/hire shop. If they're your groups' own bikes, you can start to assess how well your group know their bikes as well as looking for potential issues before they arise. Simple things like tightening loose bolts to avoid things falling off, or inflating tyres without enough air in that can lead to wheel damage or snake bite punctures.

The M check works well as a system for checking bikes over. For full details of how to perform this check and any adjustments necessary, see chapter 8.

Riding the trails

One way of managing groups at trail centres is to give them a short section to ride at their own pace with predetermined meet-up points (numbered marker posts are helpful). This allows your group the freedom to ride at their own pace, and allows plenty of space between riders so you are not strung out in one long snake along a trail. This is generally a better way of managing a group, and allows other trail centre users to pass by sensibly without having to overtake lots of people at once or get mingled with your group when they approach sections unsuitable for overtaking. This approach does however have its drawbacks, in that you are unlikely to be able to see your whole group at all times, and they may miss the stopping point causing the group to become separated. If you do need to ride as a big group, try to organise a single file system, with verbal commands or messages being passed form the back to the front or vice versa. In this formation it is important to warn people ahead of you of overtaking riders - usually a shout of 'trail' can be passed up the line fairly quickly so the group can be aware of, and give way to, other riders. Although not always advisable (depending on the section of trail you're on) it is good manners to give way to smaller groups and individuals if you are on the trail with a bigger group.

Sessioning a section

Generally this is not a good idea on part of a trail at a trail centre, which is why they often have skills areas to develop specific aspects of riding. However if you really do need to use a particular feature, and the trail is not too busy, there are a few important points to consider.

- How will you warn approaching riders that your group is at that feature - either stationary or observing the group? A marker of some sort or a lookout person is helpful here to shout a warning to both oncoming riders and the group.
- Is there a suitable place for the group to observe your demo or each other at that feature? If not you should find somewhere else to develop that skill.
- How will your riders get back to the start of the section? Ideally by pushing/riding back along the trail you're working on. Try to avoid cutting new paths/tracks into the surrounding area. Again if its really too tricky to do this without causing a major impact on the surrounding area or is just plain dangerous to go off the trail, then you need to find anther section, to use.

Repairs and accidents

Dealing with accidents and repairs (covered in chapters 8 and 9) has extra significance at a trail centre. The advantage of being on a marked trail is that you can usually identify where you are when sending for help, and also that help tends not to be too far away. The disadvantage is that a trail accident can very quickly accumulate into a multiple accident if you don't warn other riders of the incident. If you have to stop for a mechanical issue, try to get your group off the trail and in a safe place. Also think about where you are going to position yourself to best carry out the repair (or first aid if it's an accident) and manage the rest of your group. A fairly widely accepted practice is to send one of your group (or go yourself if you have time) a little further up the trail and put an upturned bike (wheels in the air) by the track as a warning sign to other riders that there is a hazard ahead. Alternatively a person/lookout can also do a good job of warning others. If you need to send for help it's a good idea to send a couple of people together with a map that they can understand. Hopefully you will have planned and checked out the emergency route back to the centre as well, so can direct the messengers where to go. Many trail centres now have emergency routes marked on the way marker posts as well. If you ring for outside help (especially if you're calling an ambulance) make sure you let the trail centre office or headquarters know too so they can direct the emergency services to where you are. They may also be able to provide help in the interim.

Skills development areas

These offer a great and usually relatively safe environment to practice or develop skills (as the name implies!). If you have a group it is often necessary to phone ahead and book so as to ensure you are not impacting other riders. Some centres charge for this facility, but many do not, and simply want to know how many other people can use the skills area safely. If you're unsure of the arrangements it's best to ask (when you're riding the trails yourself to check out if they're suitable), or give the centre a ring before turning up.

Photo 4.3: A typical trail centre route - flowing singletrack through the forest - Brechfa, Wales

Photo 4.4: Skill development, Coed Llandegla

5. Riding Skills

Smith's Combe, Quantocks

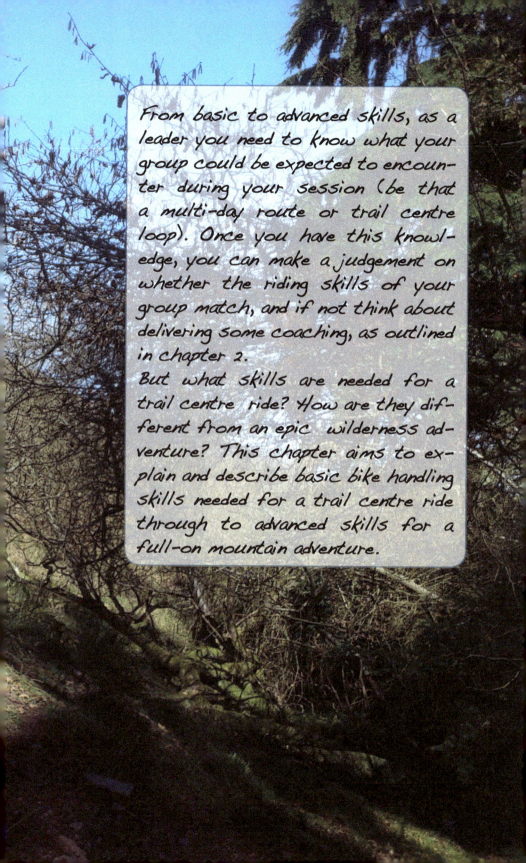

From basic to advanced skills, as a leader you need to know what your group could be expected to encounter during your session (be that a multi-day route or trail centre loop). Once you have this knowledge, you can make a judgement on whether the riding skills of your group match, and if not think about delivering some coaching, as outlined in chapter 2.

But what skills are needed for a trail centre ride? How are they different from an epic wilderness adventure? This chapter aims to explain and describe basic bike handling skills needed for a trail centre ride through to advanced skills for a full-on mountain adventure.

Riding Skills

Whilst there are many resources demonstrating a wide variety of mountain bike skills, this chapter is solely concerned with those that will be needed by a leader or their group for an adventure on their bikes. It doesn't cover anything in the way of trials skills, or trick moves, as such skills, and coaching such skills, are beyond the scope of this book. The skills covered here are specifically tailored to being able to ride a route - be that as part of a trail centre or wilderness adventure, and, in conjunction with chapter 2, how to teach and coach riders in developing the skills that will allow them to ride further, longer and harder routes.

Each skill is described, and then broken down into component parts. The skills are ordered so that the foundation skills appear first, followed by the intermediate skills, ending the chapter with the more advanced skills.

Bike set up

Key to being able to master all the skills to be described in this chapter is good bike set up, making sure you are as comfortable as possible and that the contact points between you and your bike are in the right places. Even with hired bikes it is possible to make a few small tweaks to the bikes once you've picked them up so that they fit each rider well.

Assuming that you have the right size bike (most hire shops will want rider height as a guide to what size bike to give each rider) the first and most obvious thing to adjust is the saddle. The problem is that unless you have a dropper post (highly unlikely on hired bikes) you will need to adjust the saddle height many times during the ride. This means it's a really good idea to get your group confident with the mechanical process and to understand exactly how high the saddle should be for any given section of trail.

As a guide to correct saddle height, stand the rider next to the bike and roughly adjust the height of the saddle so it is level with their hip. Once they sit on the bike, the leg should be almost (but not quite) fully extended at the lowest part of the pedal strike (with the crank vertical and the pedal closest to the ground). There should be a very small bend (an athletic bend) in the knee and its likely that the rider will just be able to touch the ground on tiptoes. Any shorter, and the rider will not be able ride at maximum efficiency as their leg will not fully extend during pedalling, and any higher and they will not be able to touch the ground if they need to, and may over extend the knee too.

Brake levers can be adjusted also, to accommodate different size hands. First of all the level should not be completely horizontal or for that matter vertical but at an angle comfortable to reach when the hand is gripping the handlebar in the riding position (see photo 5.1). To alter this just loosen the retaining bolts for the brake and angle it until it feels comfortable for the rider - ideally the wrist and arm will be in a straight line. Brake lever reach can also be adjusted on some brakes using a thumb screw or screw to wind the lever closer or further from the bar, for bigger or smaller hands. This is really important if you are riding with young people as they may not be able to reach the brake lever without releasing their thumb from under the bar, thus much reducing grip. Shifters can also be adjusted in the same way, although on some systems such as Avid's matchmaker the brakes and shifter are fixed to the same mount on the handlebars so they adjust together.

Photo 5.1: Brake levers set up correctly allowing the arm to remain in a straight line to the lever.

The Mountain Bike Leader's Handbook

Gear selection and changing

Before getting your group to practice shifting gears, its also a good idea to check that the shifter is actually puling enough (and not too much) cable through to operate the derailleur. If you hear a rattling sound as gears are changed that's an indication that there is a bit too much cable being pulled when with one click of the shifter (this is the same for trigger or grip shifters). You need to loosen the cable by turning the cable housing nut (usually the plastic bit where the cable housing meets the shifter body) a quarter turn clockwise. If this doesn't eliminate the problem, repeat until it does. If the gears do not change when the shifter is clicked then you need to do the opposite as you want more tension/shorter cable to pull the chain across the cassette further. This procedure is the same for both front and rear mechanisms (derailleurs), but it is more often a fault with the rear mech that causes a problem in shifting.

Once you know the gear shifters are working smoothly you can work on the skill of shifting to the correct gear for the terrain you are riding. Key points to note when you are teaching this skill are:

- Anticipate the change you will need and shift slightly before you think you'll need to change gear
- Continue to pedal as you change gear (cranks should always be moving forward when you change otherwise there is a risk the chain will jam in the derailleur or come off.)
- Although you are turning the cranks, try to exert as little force as possible when you make the change (too much force can cause the chain to jump off the cassette or even snap - if it starts making a heavy clicking sound when you change gear you're putting too much force on it)
- Use a lower gear (bigger cogs/sprockets at the back, easier to pedal) for going uphill, and a higher gear (smaller cogs/sprockets at the back for going downhill). If you need to move across chain rings at the front (assuming you have a bike with 2 or 3 chain rings at the front) then do that separately from changing at the rear, not at the same time.

- Try to avoid having the chain on the biggest sprocket at the back and the biggest one at the front, or the smallest one at the front and smallest one at the back, as this makes the chain run with a significant diagonal force on it (look at the chain from behind the rear wheel and you will see the chain going at a diagonal instead of straight from the cassette to the chain rings.)

Photo 5.2: A diagonal chain line puts excess strain on the chain and can lead to it snapping.

As a leader it is worth getting your group to ride around the introduction area to assess how well they can change gear, as this will be really important to know so you can set the rest of the session at the appropriate level. If you are going on a longer rider, it's well worth spending some time getting your group to be able to shift smoothly, as rough shifting is likely to cause mechanical problems as you go, with dropped chains and even broken chains taking time to fix and put back on.

Moving around the bike

In order to get the most from a modern trail bike, you can't ride it sat on the saddle for the whole time. Moving your body weight around the bike will greatly improve your ability to get the bike to go where you want it to, and do what you want it to do.

When riding uphill you need to stay seated for as long as possible to keep your weight over the back wheel and maintain grip. You will need to move forwards on the saddle so you are right on the nose as the gradient you are riding gets steeper to avoid the front end lifting and causing a loss of control. Dropping your chest low over the top tube can also help with keeping the front end down.

When not pedalling over rough ground, or descending you need to get up out of the saddle and get into the neutral position (photo 5.3). This is with your pedals level, your arms and knees slightly bent (to absorb any impacts) and your weight above the front of the saddle (roughly in the middle of the bike). As you start to go downhill move your weight backwards, keeping your knees bent. For very steep downhill sections or rollable drop offs, you will need your weight right over the back wheel, but remember to always come back to the neutral position when you can.

Braking

Braking effectively involves more than just grabbing the brake levers and squeezing as hard as possible. You should try to avoid skidding at all times, as during a skid you are still moving but with the brakes on, so you have no control over your speed, and directional control is reduced too

Photo 5.3: The neutral position

as your tyres aren't gripping the ground anymore. As with gear changes, it's important to anticipate when you might need to brake - if you're coming in to a corner too fast, scrub the speed off before you hit the corner, not during. Use both brakes together for the most effective braking, and when braking from a high speed, you'll need to move your weight back slightly from the neutral position to counteract the momentum your body will have gained. If you grab too much front brake you may go over the bars as the bike slows and stops but you don't, and if you grab too much rear brake you will skid and possibly end up on the floor as a result of the bike sliding away from under you. On slightly longer descents you may want to feather your brakes to control speed but not stop completely. This involves gently squeezing the brake levers so that you apply force evenly and gently to remove just the right amount of speed, but not too much. If you do this over a short section the drag you create allows you to control your speed. However, on longer sections you need to constantly squeeze the brakes gently and release the lever (this is feathering) to allow the pads and rotor to cool for a fraction of a second before re-applying the brakes. The longer the descent, the more feathering of the brakes you need to do as hot brake pads and discs are less effective then cold ones. On really long descents if you are not confident at going full tilt for the whole thing, you may have to stop at stages to allow your brakes to cool (and probably rest your forearms too!).

Track stand

The track stand is a useful manoeuvre to master and is a good practice of balance. Basically you are trying to stand up on the pedals in more or less the neutral position without moving forwards of backwards at all. To do this you will need to turn the handlebar and hence front wheel so they are almost at right angles to the normal straight line running position and keep both brakes on. You then need to move your body (not the bike) to balance in the upright position for as long as possible. Practising this gets you used to the feel of moving around with the bike relatively

Photo 5.4: The track stand

stationary under you, and also allows you to get to grips with exactly where the balance point of the bike is. In the early stages you may need to release the brakes ever so slightly for a few cm of movement to help keep you balanced.

Riding uphill

In riding uphill there are two important factors to think about. Firstly keeping the front of the bike down as it will want to rise and go off line. Secondly keeping the power going through the rear wheel at just the right level to keep you moving, but not spin out and lose grip. There comes a point where the two are virtually irreconcilable, but up to that point you have a good chance of keeping going if you think about your most effective body position. You need to be in a low gear (easier to pedal) and move your weight forward so you are perched on the nose of the saddle. Don't stand up (yet) otherwise you will lose grip with the rear tyre and spin out. Staying on the saddle keeps the majority of your body weight acting through the seat tube and stays to keep the rear tyre glued down. You need to drop your chest towards the top tube to add some of your weight over the front of the bike to try to keep the front tyre in contact with the ground too. When it finally gets too much to continue or your thighs and glutes are burning, you will need to stand up but don't just get up and stamp on the pedals. You need to moderate how much power you put down, as being in a low gear and now moving your weight forward (by the act of standing on the pedals) you are likely spin out. Instead try to stand up with your weight over the saddle and ease off on the power slightly to maintain grip. As you get moving in this position then you can increase the power you are putting through the pedals. When a steep hill beats a rider its is often because they have lost control (front end washes out) or lost traction (rear wheel spins out). Trying to keep the balance between power and grip and managing exactly where your weight is, is key to riding steep uphill sections successfully.

Riding downhill

For downhill riding on moderately steep ground, the key is to anticipate and try to ride smoothly, with flow. You need to be up in the neutral position ready to move your weight around to cope with any obstacles you encounter. As the ground gets steeper you will need to move more of your body backwards, to keep the rear tyre gripping the ground and ensure you don't overbalance over the bars. Stand up and bend your knees with your heels dropped on the pedals, and arms slightly bent (elbows out) ready to absorb anything the suspension doesn't deal with, and keep you balanced. If you have to turn, look where you want to go and your body and bike will follow. Try to judge the right amount of speed that will allow you to feel comfortable going over obstacles or round corners before you get to them and brake accordingly. The faster you go, the further ahead you need to scan the trail, as you have less time to deal with things. Try to avoid getting sucked into 'front wheel vision' (a bit like tunnel vision but more dangerous), as this will help you see things in plenty of time to react to them. Allow the bike to move under you and try not to hang on too tightly other wise your arms will ache and you won't be able to tighten your grip when you really need to. Ideally your head should stay fairly still with your body and the bike moving underneath it. Your head leads the way and everything else follows.

Riding off camber

Off camber sections are those that you ride across a slope, so the tendency is for you to lean into the slope to feel safer. If you ride like this you will be putting your weight (and hence centre of gravity) off to one side (the uphill side) and the bike will probably slide down the slope and away from you. Many people do this with their uphill foot raised to avoid a pedal strike and their downhill foot low with their downhill leg straight. This restricts your mobility on the bike and if it does start to slide away

Photo 5.5: A photo montage of riding a flowing, undulating trail. Notice how Jonny keeps his head and upper body level above the bike, allowing it to move beneath him and absorb the uneven trail, whilst keeping his weight balanced over the middle of the bike. He is in a slightly lower position than the neutral position, so he can move his hips and hence bodyweight to stay in balance and also push with his legs where he needs to pump the trail to gain momentum. He looks where he wants to go, not down at his wheel and leads with his head.

from you, the only way to correct it is to actually steer up the slope slightly, which may well have you running off line/where you want to go.

A better approach is to keep your pedals level and twist your hips so they face up the slope, with your body weight slightly off to the down slope side of your bike. This means your weight is pushing the tyres in to the slope, giving grip, and if the bike does slide, its slides underneath you (not away from you) allowing you to stay in control. It's counter-intuitive to ride in this way but if you practice this on a section of off camber trail you will see and feel the benefits.

Flowing singletrack

The key to riding the flowing singletrack, which is a major feature of modern trail centres, is a smooth flow to your movement around the gentle curves, to preserve speed and minimise the effort you need to put in. In order to do this you need to concentrate on looking well ahead and steering by moving your body and in particular your hips and head and not pulling the bike round by levering on the bars too much. If you think about how a slalom skier looks ahead and uses their head and then hips to initiate and then follow a turn, that gives you a good picture for the body shape you should adopt to ride smoothly on flowing singletrack. At its best, it should feel smooth and effortless and will allow you carry speed even on shallow gradients. When you steer with your hips your body weight automatically moves slightly outside the top tube and helps maintain grip by gently pushing the bike into the corner, adding grip, and as you come out of the turn you get a slingshot effect adding momentum to your bike without actually having to pedal. This is emphasised to its maximum when the corners are bermed (see below for good berm riding technique).

Rollers

Rollers are really rolling undulations in a trail, often featured in trail centre routes. They allow a skilled rider to gain speed without pedaling, by pumping as they ride through the rollers. This is the first skill that requires you to be able to weight and unweight your bike, which sounds difficult to do and is difficult to describe. Basically, when you are weighting the bike you are pushing down through your legs (and to some extent your arms) to force the bike into the trail and feel 'heavy'. Unweighting is the opposite; you are trying to make the bike feel light underneath you by relaxing and keeping your weight as evenly distributed as possible. Of course you can't defy gravity so there will be some weight on the bike, but the movement in weighting and unweighting is about adding or removing extra compression force on the bike frame by pushing (or not) with your legs (and to a lesser extent arms - see photo 5.6).

Pumping a roller (gaining speed from a small trail feature without pedaling) involves unweighting the bike on the way up the roller, and then weighting the bike on the downslope. Concentrate on being as light as possible as you go up the roller, and as you reach the top, push the front wheel gently away from you by straightening your arms slightly, and at the same time pushing down with your legs. Doing this means you lose as little speed as possible going up the bump, and gain as much as possible on the way down. Skilled riders can gain significant speed on sections of rollers, although they tend to be found on the more easily graded trails. Once you have mastered riding rollers and gaining speed, you can use the pump technique on less smooth, more technical sections of trail to the same ends, but combined with other skills to manage rougher more technical trail features, such as those on red or black graded trails.

Doubles

A double is really two rollers close together, so that if you're riding at a decent speed there isn't really time to do anything in between each crest. You need to employ the same technique as for pumping a roller, but this time there are two options depending on how fast you are going. If you are going really fast then you can treat the double as one roller, and unweight the bike for the first up, the first down and the second up

The Mountain Bike Leader's Handbook

before weighting the bike on the second downslope. You need to extend and then contract your arms as you go down then up in between the crests but remain unweighted during this period. This will help you gain speed and also absorb the tendency of the bike to buck up underneath you (there is more tendency to buck in the rear end of a hardtail as it's only your legs absorbing the shock). If you are going slightly slower then

Photo sequence 5.6 (opposite): Tom riding a double and pumping for speed.
1. Tom is at the top of the first of a pair of doubles. He is winding up to push down with his arms and legs as soon as his weight hits the top of the rise.
2. Tom is on the way up the second rise and stands up to unweight the bike on the up slope.
3. Tom has crested the second rise and is now winding up again to pump (push) down the slope and gain speed.
4. Tom pushes down on the down slope, extending his arms and legs to force the bike into the trail and hence gain as much speed from the downslope as possible. A close look reveals he has forced the front end down so far that the rear wheel is actually in the air (it would be better to have it still in contact and gripping, but this demonstrates how much force he is using to pump the downslope).
5. Now he is rising up on the first part of the second double in the sequence and is just starting to move from unweighting the bike to being ready to pump the downslope.
6. At the end of the sequence, Tom is extending his arms and legs to pump the downslope (albeit not as much of a slope as the first double in the sequence).

you'll need to make some movement in the dip between the double to maintain speed and balance. As you crest the top of the first roller, weight your bike (but only until you're about halfway down the roller). The easiest way to do this is to push the bike away from you by extending your arms. As you get into the dip between the crests of the double, you need to already be unweighting the bike and pulling your arms towards you so they are bent again as you go up the second crest. Once you get to the top, weight the bike and gently extend your arms to gain maximum momentum as you leave the feature.

Photo 5.7: George riding a boardwalk - notice how he maintains the neutral position and stays in the middle of the boards

Boardwalk riding

A common feature of trail centres is wooden structures, the lowest level of which is planks on a slightly raised framework, often there to avoid boggy or poorly drained sections. Higher from the ground or cambered sections tend to be known as Northshore (from the Northshore area of Vancouver where they first became popular) and are covered later in the section. Riding boardwalk is relatively simple but bear in mind that wood gets slippery when wet (even if it has some wire mesh nailed over the top of the wood). Try to ride as straight as possible a path along a wooden boardwalk, and avoid sharp movements such as reactive steering or brak-

Photo sequence 5.8 (opposite): Tom (red) and Paul (blue) log hopping. Initially they both sink down to compress the fork and bend their arms and legs, ready for the explosive phase.
By the second picture, Tom has exploded upwards with his whole body, arms and legs straight and taken the bike with him as he leaps upwards. Paul on the other hand has pulled up and back on the bars (see bent arms) which has also pulled his body forward over the front wheel.
By the third photo, Tom has landed by pushing the bike gently away from him in mid air (straightening his arms) whilst still maintaining forward

momentum as he leapt up whilst in motion. He lands on the logs ready to pedal on. Paul however has hung up on the edge of the logs as he could only pull up so far (due to arm length) and as he was pulling up and back on the bars all that really happened was the front wheel pivoted up around the rear axle so he has lost his forward momentum and stalled.

ing. Riding boardwalk smoothly tests your ability to anticipate how the bike will behave on the trail ahead of you, and move your body weight accordingly. Getting it wrong will mean the bike quickly slips away from under you and a painful landing will follow! Try to maintain grip at all times - don't brake suddenly, don't steer sharply, keep your weight in the neutral position and only pedal if you really need to - sit down if you can to pedal - and get into a slightly higher gear than you would if it were a firm section of trail to reduce the chance of slipping out when applying pedal power.

Front wheel lift (log hop)

This is the first of the more complex skills that most riders need to learn, and is really useful in riding along rough trails, smoothly. If you can lift the front wheel of the bike, you can pop it up and over small obstacles such as small logs and roots, or rock steps. It is also a foundation move for the more advanced techniques such as bunnyhopping, or trials skills such as the manual.

Although eventually you should aim to lift the front wheel and continue riding smoothly over the obstacle, in learning it is helpful to break down the skill into a number of stages.

Firstly select a mid-range gear so you can pedal but not too easily. As you are riding along you need to stand up into the neutral position. Then, lean forward and push down with your arms so that the suspension fork compresses. Bend your legs slightly at the same time. As the fork responds and starts to push back up, straighten your arms and legs so you are in effect springing up into a small jump. The front of the bike will come up with you as you naturally stand up tall at the apex of your spring - you shouldn't be pulling up on the bars really hard as this works to lift the wheel a small amount, but not much, and leaves you out of balance for the landing as your weight is committed to moving backwards as you yank on the bars. Better is to gain height by springing up with your legs and allowing the bars to be pulled up as your arms move along with the rest of your body. Most people can spring up higher than they can pull up (as your arms can only bend so much), and if you've gone up (instead of back), when you land you will still be in the neutral position ready for the next trail obstacle or feature.

Small drop offs

Small (meaning less than about 30cm) drop offs are commonly encountered on blue routes, and offer the opportunity to learn and practice skills which can then be transferred to bigger drop offs found on red and black trails. The easiest way to ride a drop off of this height is to roll down it. To do this as you come to the lip (edge) of the drop off (in the neutral position), extend your arms and push the front of the bike away from you, down the drop. This naturally makes the bike move down, staying in contact with the trail and means your weight shifts to the back of the bike. This is not because you've leant back but simply the bike has moved under you. As the front wheel hits the flat or down slope, bend your arms again, bringing the bike back under your body so you return to the neutral position. If you try this by pulling up or leaning backwards then when you land, you are in a really unstable position and may well topple off the back of the bike. At the least your front wheel will be unweighted so will have little or no grip and be out of your control.

As you get better and smoother at riding small drop offs, and become more confident of your ability to land under control, you can increase the speed that you approach the drop off. As you get faster, you need to push the front of the bike less hard (i.e. not as far forward) as you go off the lip of the drop. You also need to bend your legs to absorb the impact of the landing (you'll need to bend more on a flat landing than on a downslope, but a downslope landing requires you to land in a balanced position). As you get quicker at doing this you will feel that both wheels leave the ground as you go off the lip, with the bike staying more or less horizontal in the air, so both wheels can land at the same time and you can absorb the impact evenly through your legs.

Rutted tracks

Ruts (deep, narrow channels worn by water or lots of tyres passing through them) can prove tricky if you're not expecting them or don't know how to ride them. Generally my advice is to stay out of ruts as you can't always predict how far or deep they'll run. If you do find yourself riding in a rut then try to keep your pedals level (to avoid striking them on the sides of the rut) and steer straight to follow where ever the rut goes. Get out of it when possible, either by steering gently up and out (if it's not too deep) or by side hopping when you're stable (providing you can side hop). You need to maintain speed, as pedalling in a rut is really hard to do without clipping a pedal and knocking yourself off to one side, or off the bike altogether. If you need to move your weight around, do so by pointing your hips and moving them to one side or the other as opposed to leaning the bike over or your whole body away from the centre line of the rut. That way the bike stays balanced and running true in the direction you want it to go. This is also a really useful technique if you are riding a very thin course, such as along a log or plank bridge.

Muddy sections

Muddy sections, sometimes including puddles are common features and the simple rule for riding them is steer straight and stay in the neutral position. You are unlikely to be able to grip in a muddy area, so pedaling or braking are just going to lead to skids, slides and generally being out of control. Stay in the neutral position so you are ready to move your weight back if you slow dramatically as you enter the mud, otherwise as the bike loses momentum rapidly and your body doesn't, you end up going over the bars and getting a face full of mud as well.

Water crossing and deep puddles

Similar to riding muddy sections, riding through water or deeper, bigger puddles requires some care to avoid falling off. If you attack water more than about 10cm deep too fast, the drag of the water on the bike will slow you too rapidly and you'll stall (and have to put your feet down) or fall off sideways. The key is to carry some momentum into the water but be in a mid-range to higher gear so that if/when you need to pedal you can apply some measured power without the back wheel just spinning. The sensible thing to do before riding through any water is to stop before it, have a look at how deep it is and whether there are unseen obstacles to avoid before you actually try and ride through. If you are fording a river or stream, look at the exit point and check that it is rideable and not too steep to knock you backwards just when you think you've made it. Also beware of the speed of the water. Even what looks like a slow current can knock your front wheel off line as you enter the water meaning you're out of control from the start. If in doubt with water crossings or really deep/big/unknown puddles, get off and push.

Rooty sections – up

When riding over any roots, the most important factor is the angle at which you cross them. Ideally you would cross directly at ninety degrees to the root so that the time your wheels are in contact with the roots is the shortest possible. In practice this is rarely possible, so you often need to compromise between hitting the roots at right angles and staying on your intended line.

When tackling roots uphill the biggest problem you have is the lack of grip offered by the rounded shape and woody nature of the roots. They tend not to have bark on, so are very smooth which makes them really tricky if the ground is wet. As well as trying to plot a course that allows you to cross the rooty section as quickly as possible, you need to maximise grip. Do this by remaining seated to keep the rear wheel weighted, steer straight to keep the front wheel in contact and avoid braking. If you need to pedal, choose a slightly higher gear than the slope looks like it needs, so you don't over-do the power and spin out. If the rooty section is part of a longer climb, it's worth trying to give yourself a boost just before so you can coast over it before pedaling again.

Rooty sections – down

Tackling a rooty section riding downhill is slightly more simple than going up hill, but the sample principles apply. You want to be off the roots as quickly as possible and maintain grip. You should be more or less in the neutral position with your weight slightly towards the back of the bike. Ride as straight a course as possible over the roots, and avoid steering, otherwise your front wheel is likely to wash out as it loses grip.

An approach for those who are more confident is to use the first root as a kicker and combine the bump with a small log hop (front wheel raise) or better still bunnyhop to jump over the roots, thereby avoiding the grip issues altogether. This takes practice and requires you to combine the skills of descending and the log hop/bunnyhop. In practice it is the most efficient way of dealing with shorter sections, but be sure you're not landing on more roots as you will likely slide out of control on your landing. For longer rooty sections the only option is to ride them out as smoothly as you can, with as little steering as possible.

Berms

A berm, or sculpted corner is really just a roller on its side, and as such there is a lot in common between riding a roller and riding (or railing) a berm. In terms of line choice its is better to aim to go high on the way in and low on the way out, to maximise the speed that can be gained.

As with the roller technique, you need to approach the berm in the neutral position, and as you enter the berm unweight the bike so it feels light under you. As you get to the apex of the corner (when you feel the turning force is at its maximum), weight the bike by pushing down with your legs and also steer down the face of the berm slightly, and you will gain speed.

The real difference in railing a berm to riding a roller is the sideways orientation of the berm means that in order to maintain grip, you need to lean the bike over to maximise both the grip and the force you can apply as you weight the bike coming out of the turn. In order to turn smoothly, turn your hips to the inside of the corner, and look at the exit. As you do so you need to lean the bike (and yourself slightly) over towards the inside of the turn. The faster you go, the more you need to lean, and conversely you can only lean over at speed as the centrifugal force pulling you up and to the outside of the corner is what supports you as you lean over. A high speed entry, steep lean and powerful weighting on the way out of a berm allows you to gain speed (not lose it as may be the case with flat corners). Whatever you do, don't brake in the berm - decide the speed you are comfortable with before hand and apply the brakes gently to get there, then let them off and concentrate on your body position. As has been mentioned in an earlier chapter, berms are one way trail centre designers add speed to trails and try to minimise the creation of braking bumps when the trail needs to change direction.

Photo 5.9: Railing a berm - notice the bike leant over, hips turned towards the exit and head turned looking ahead, eyes focussed on the exit

Table tops

Table tops tend to be features of trail centres, and there are not many that are naturally occurring. They tend to be the starting point for learning to jump and get a bike airborne, and as such require a combination of skills. The key thing in riding a table top and successfully getting some air is timing.

A table top is exactly what is says; a flat, raised area of trail with a steep up slope and distinct (but maybe not so steep) downslope. As you ride towards the table top, you need to be in the neutral position, and be ready to perform the same sort of move as for the log hop and start of the bunnyhop. As you hit the upslope, push down with your legs and bend your arms and legs. As you hit the lip of the table top, you need to explode upwards (literally jumping up), bringing the bike with you. The upslope and lip of the table top will mean that you carry on higher than you would normally with a lop hop or bunnyhop. In the air, push the bars gently away from you to level out the bike and bend your knees and arms to allow the bike to continue to rise under you and also be ready to land. As you start to descend, extend your arms and legs to make the bike meet the ground (as opposed to you and the bike hitting the ground). As soon as contact is made, start to bend your arms and legs to absorb the impact force.

The faster you approach the table top, the further you are likely to go, so at a certain speed you need to be prepared to land on the downslope. In order to do this you need to push the bike away further in the air so that both wheels can still land at the same time. Cut outs (see p87) should only be attempted once you can clear a tabletop and land on the downslope.

Rocky sections – up

In some ways, rocky sections are similar to rooty sections in that you need to cross the sharp, hard edges of rocks at right angles as you do roots. However, rocky sections tend to go on for longer and therefore present extra problems when riding up them.

Look for the line of least resistance to attack. This may need you to go up some square edges (use the log hop skill described earlier) or weave around larger rocks. Thus, you have to maintain all the poise and skill of the usual uphill ride (sitting down, arms bent and chest low), whilst steering, sometimes hopping up and keeping an even allocation of power to match how much grip you will have. Beware of turning too much (you tend to lose grip) or just ploughing straight up, as you lose speed rapidly. Tactics are the key to conquering a rocky climb - look out for a line well ahead of actually getting to the rocky climb, decide where you're going to go, and then stick to that line as best as possible. Keep in a low gear and keep the cranks turning if possible (avoiding pedal strikes). You will need to move your weight around constantly to maintain both balance and effective forward motion, and concentrate on the exit point of the section.

Rocky sections - down

On the way down, rocky sections present challenges in staying on line (and for some, staying on the bike!), as they tend to bounce you around and if you're not careful dictate where you go instead of you steering and controlling the line.

As you approach the section, pick your line (and if it isn't already, drop your saddle down as far as it'll go so it is out of the way). This maybe the line of least resistance or if you are confident enough to hop or jump parts of the section you may be able to use early rocks as kickers to help lift you over the rest (but make sure you have a smooth landing spot picked out). You need to be up on your pedals but with your weight over the back of the bike (the steeper the section, the further back you need to have your weight). Try and stay loose - on the grips and over the bike - let the bike move under you but keep your weight fairly central (laterally). Obviously you need to hold on so you don't get bounced off the bike altogether, but if you try to be as light as possible with your hands in particular you will avoid arm pump, a common problem on longer rocky sections. Try to ride as straight as possible as steering can cause you to lose grip or hit rocks with the side of the wheel which will knock you off line or even damage a spoke. If you can avoid braking then all the better, but if you do feel things running away from you, brake in the smoother/less hard edged sections to try to maintain some semblance of grip.

When you are developing your skills it is well worth sessioning a section of rocky descent - to try out the different lines and associate them with what you can see from above on the trail, and to see which are faster or easier to ride (not always the same thing).

Steep slopes - up

Similar to riding up hill in general, steep slopes require good skills and fitness to surmount. The same principles apply in terms of trying to keep the front wheel down, but with some weight over the back wheel to avoid losing grip. When the slope gets to a point when you can no longer pedal sitting down you have to stand up to put more force on the pedals and hopefully power you up the incline. However, be warned that most people can only manage this stand up sprint type technique for a short period, so pick your spot and get the timing right - a quick burst can be enough to get you over the steepest section of a long slope, but try standing for too long and you'll either get tired, or more probably lose grip.

You need to stand on the pedals as you turn them, leaning forward but with your weight still over the saddle. Many people make the mistake of standing forward on the pedals over the top tube. This unweights the rear end of the bike, so although the front stays down, the rear tyre spins out and you end up stalling. This skill is really important (but not much fun) to practice so you can keep going and overcome steep sections on the routes you're riding.

Steep slopes - down

On the way down very steep sections you need to ride in the same way as a smaller drop off. Get your weight right over the back of the bike, nice and low, and straighten your arms a little so you are pushing or guiding the bike in front of you. The steeper the slope, the more in front of you than underneath you, the bike is. Your limit is when your backside is just off touching the back wheel - but be warned if you're on a full-sus bike as a large bump could knock you painfully from underneath - and will inevitably knock you off the bike too.

Drop offs

Larger drop offs (larger than abut 30cm as considered above) require a lot more confidence and commitment to ride successfully, and it is well worth honing your skills on smaller drops, as the consequences get more serious as the drop off height increases. To ride larger drop offs (which are not rollable) you need to attack the lip at speed, (in the neutral position), and stand up slightly, pushing down with your legs as you hit the lip. Push the bike away from you gently whilst you are in the air so as to level out the wheels, and brace yourself for landing. When you land, bend your knees to absorb the impact. Landing flat puts far more force on your legs, so if you can, choose a drop off that has a sloping landing. If this is the case you need to push the bike away further in the air so that the wheels are virtually parallel with the slope you will land on, thus allowing you to land with both wheels touching down together if possible. In practice you can usually get away with the rear wheel landing fractionally before the front, but too early and you'll tip off the back of the bike.

Cut outs

A cut out is really just a table top with out the top. It is effectively the upslope and downslope only with nothing in the middle. It should be obvious that if you don't make it and clear the gap, you'll land in it and almost certainly end of off the bike and probably hurt as well. The technique is exactly the same as for tabletops, but you must have enough speed and commitment to the feature to clear it and land on the downslope. To get more distance on your table top jumps (to prepare you for cut outs) you should look to increase speed of approach (but not so fast that you're out of control) and work on getting the timing right so you explode upwards just as the bike follows you off the lip of the upslope. Land as for downslope landing with the wheel parallel to the ground so they touch down together.

Northshore

Northshore sections are really just bigger, higher and longer boardwalks, that are so named from their popularity on trails in the Northshore area of Vancouver, British Columbia. The same principles apply as for riding boardwalks, with bigger consequences if you get it wrong. They may also incorporate bermed corners, narrow sections, step ups of downs (like small drop offs) and as such require you to combine the skills for riding boardwalk with those other trail feature skills. There is something thrilling about whizzing along a narrow ribbon of woodwork at somewhere above head height in a forest that gives you a totally different perspective on the trees around you. But don't contemplate too much otherwise you'll be off the edge to a painful landing!

Carrying your bike

There will be times, especially if you're out on natural trails and in the wilderness or on a mountain route where it is just impossible to continue riding, no matter how good you are. Sometimes magazine articles and guidebooks refer to these sections as hike-a-bike, but there is a skill to carrying a bike to make it as least uncomfortable as possible. Here, hardtails are the easiest to transport as they tend to be lighter, and have more space in the front triangle to get your arms/shoulders into a good load bearing position.

To carry your bike as efficiently and comfortably as possible (bear in mind they're not designed to be carried so it's never that comfortable), lay it on the ground and bend down to pick it up with one hand on the uppermost bar end and the other on the pedal facing out towards you. Lift and and as you do so, swing the bike around your shoulders (as if you were putting on a jacket) to bring the bike to rest with the top tube across your shoulders (but not quite square on them). Your hand on the bar end can then adjust the position of the bike (with some careful shrugging also needed) so that it feels balanced with the majority of the weight on your shoulders. The balance point and exact orientation of the bike will be governed by the frame design (shape) and material/spec of the bike (weight), so it is worth practising this with your bike before you have to do it for real. Be careful not to get blown over if you are carrying your bike this way as your centre of gravity is now much higher than usual, especially if you are wearing a rucksack carrying kit.

Bunnyhop

The bunnyhop is a useful progression from the log hop in that it allows you to get both wheels up and over an obstacle to maintain speed and flow. The set up and first part of the bunnyhop are exactly the same as the log hop. Push down with your legs, bend your arms and then explode upwards, straightening your arms and legs as you rise and then bending them as the bike follows up underneath. A bunnyhop requires you to actively lift the rear end of the bike just after you have lifted the front wheel - so both wheels don't quite go up together but the rear follows the front. To achieve this lift, when you are in the air you need to do two things. Push the bike way from you by straightening your arms (just like when riding a larger drop off) and then point your toes downwards and scoop the pedal up and behind you, which acts to lift the rear wheel. I would strongly recommend practising this with flat pedals even if you normally ride with cleats - they allow you to lift the back wheel but without developing the technique, so that when you need to hop in a real trail if your timing is even a little off the back wheel comes up too early, pushing the front wheel down meaning you are more likely to land front wheel heavy and go over the bars. This artificial pull is not possible with flats, so I think

Photo sequence 5.10 (opposite): Tom bunnyhopping a log.

1. Tom prepares by getting low and bending his arms and legs, ready for an explosive leap upwards.
2. Just before he reaches the log, he pushes hard with his legs and literally jumps up into the air.
3. As he rises into the air, he scoops the pedals with his feet (toes pointing down or even backwards) to help lift the bike and get extra height.
4. Once in mid-air, Tom pushes the front of the bike away from his body by straightening his arms, and gently bends his legs allowing the rear end of the bike to come up under him, whilst maintaining forward momentum.
5. Finally he brings the bike to meet the ground, and keeps his weight low over the back of the bike with knees bent to absorb the impact and avoid being bounced off the bike or over the bars.

it's best to learn moves like this on flats and then go back to cleats once you've got them wired.

Summary

There is no requirement to be able to demonstrate these skills all perfectly before leading a group, but a good understanding of the techniques required will allow you to effectively coach riders who are technically better than you (which will be some of them). It certainly helps to be confident in what you can do, and not rest on your laurels as a leader, but push yourself when you are not leading a group - when riding on your own or with friends. Don't be afraid to get a group member to demonstrate a skill if you see that they can do it well, and especially if you're not so sure you can give a good example.

6. Navigation

Once you've planned your ride and are confident you have the right or at least permission to go where you wish to, there comes the small matter of making sure you stay on route. Some areas have well marked trails and bridleways with easy to read marker posts, but once you get off the beaten track, you will need some basic navigation skills to ensure an enjoyable mountain biking experience for you and your group.

Compass

Navigation

Whilst many volumes have been written on the subject of navigation, and thus there is a lot to cover in a single chapter, this chapter attempts to give a basic overview, along with some specific considerations for leading groups of mountain bikers. The main difference when mountain biking, compared with other activities that need land navigation skills, is the speed at which you travel, and thus what you can observe as you go along. For a more detailed look into land navigation consider having a look at some of the further reading suggested at the end of the chapter. Even if you only ever lead groups or ride at trail centres, this chapter is still worth a look through to make sure you understand the reasons and basic concepts behind navigating your way successfully.

Why navigate?

So let's consider this question first of all. Do you really need any navigation or location skills if you're at a trail centre with marker posts and man-made trails? The short answer is yes, but you use different tools to do it. Navigation is important for two main reasons. First and foremost so you don't get lost and go where you shouldn't or where you don't want to, and make it home/back to the car at the end of the route. Secondly,

> **Top Tip:**
> Always ride the route you will lead your group on beforehand. This has many benefits, some already mentioned in previous chapters. From a navigation point of view it allows you to have sight of the route and any specific navigational difficulties you may face, access restrictions and emergency escape routes should they be needed. This is even true of trail centres. Where this is not possible you need to prepare thoroughly, using all the resources available such as Google Earth, OS maps, local knowledge/info, guidebooks etc. so you have the best idea of the terrain before you get out there with your group.

if the worst happens and you need to call the emergency services they need to know where to come and find you. You may even need to navigate to a place where they can access you or get a phone signal to call them out in the first place.

The tools you use to navigate will depend upon your own preference and whereabouts you are leading/riding. However, the fall back position for any good leader is a map of the area and a compass. In the UK we are fortunate to have some excellent quality mapping available in the form of Ordnance Survey maps at various scales for the whole country, and from other companies such as Harvey's for popular areas., or mountain bike specific routes. Further afield you need to check the availability of mapping and the scale quality before you plan your ride.

Photo 6.1: The OS map collection showing some of the series and scales available. An invaluable resource in the UK.

Navigation technology

In the 21st Century there are a number of technological aids which we can use to navigate which are faster than a map and compass and have a high degree of accuracy. Since the advent of the handheld GPS, these devices have become smaller and contained more information, in much the same way as mobile phones. Small, ultra portable GPS devices are widely available and relatively well priced so they are a common sight amongst mountain bikers. Add in the fact that they can record your position, speed and some biometric data and they can rapidly appear essential equipment. This is not so, but if you do have one of these devices, or use your smart phone and one of the navigation apps, it's worth knowing a bit about how they work before trusting everything to them. Also bear in mind that whilst they may be your preference for navigation, batteries run flat, the cold curtails the abilities of many electronic circuits, and sometimes you just can't get a signal. The top models are a handheld GPS receiver and have OS or other mapping stored on a memory card so they can not only give you a grid reference with which to pinpoint your position on a map, but actually show you where you are on a display of that map in full colour. These devices are really helpful if you get lost and need to relocate yourself quickly, particularly if visibility is poor. Most offer the ability to plan your route beforehand on a PC/laptop and then upload this route to the GPS which can guide you in much the same way as in-car navigation systems do. If you are using a GPS device, then there are a few things to bear in mind to ensure it is a really useful bit of kit and not a hindrance to a good day's riding.

- Make sure it's fully charged or you're carrying spare batteries
- Keep it somewhere warm (like a chest pocket) if you're out in really cold weather - cold affects the electronics but also the battery life of lithium batteries
- Use mapping that is of an appropriate scale - I prefer 1:50000 or 1:40000 as this allows you to track progress and still take in features around you
- If possible plan the route beforehand on a PC/laptop and upload the route, along with some alternatives for emergency escapes and enforced redirections due to weather/injury/mechanical etc.
- Make sure you know how to get an actual grid reference of your position - you can't report a dot on a map display to the emergency services should you need them.

Bar mounted devices offer a good option to save having to keep stopping and getting the device out and having to hold it to see your progress. If you're using a phone with an app like Viewranger, make sure you have a way of making an emergency call as well. GPS functions are

Photo 6.2: A bike mounted GPS device with OS mapping and colour display.

high consumers of electrical power and hence a phone battery will drain quickly if it is acting as your GPS device, map display and emergency contact system. If you are keeping a GPS in your jacket pocket, make sure it's not the same pocket as your trusty back up compass, as the magnetic field generated by electrical devices can affect the accuracy of a magnetic needle (the same goes for keeping your compass next to your mobile phone).

Trail centre navigation

Navigating a trail centre route should be a more straightforward proposition than a natural route as trails are generally marked with way posts and signs to tell you which trail you are on. Many also have emergency rotes back to the centre building or help point as well, but this is no excuse for not checking out the route before you ride it with a group. It is still really important you have a map of the trail you're on, either a paper map or pdf/image stored on your phone. At worst take a photo of the trail board at the start of the route! It's also useful to have the emergency contact number for the trail centre stored in your phone in case you need to summon help, and some trail centre maps even mark on reception blackspots where there is no cell signal. Pay particular attention to the way posts as they are usually numbered, so if you do need help you can specify exactly where you are

Traditional navigation (the fall back method)

There are several different things that you need to consider when navigating with a map and compass. From a mountain biking point of view these methods are time consuming and slow down the flow when leading a group. Also consider that time taken having to stop to navigate often, will mean that you will be back later, any first aid or mechanical incidents will delay you further and you may end up getting back after dark. All the more reason to use some sort of navigation technology and pre-ride the route you'll be leading.

There are lots of things to remember when learning to navigate, and the method below is just one from many that exist, but it is one I have come to favour having taught navigation in a variety of situations to a wide range of students/clients. I find it particularly useful as it breaks down the overall task of navigation into concepts to be understood, without just giving mechanical steps which may not be fully realised.

The Five D's of Land Navigation

The model of land navigation below is a version of Chris Sweetman's[*] 4D model, that I have specifically adapted to be suitable for mountain bikers. The concepts involved in navigating when mountain biking are:

- Detection - finding out where you are
- Destination - where you want to go and how to get there
- Direction - where are you going to need to go to get to the destination and what will you encounter along the way
- Distance - how far is it to your destination
- Duration - how long will it take you to get there

So let's consider each of these concepts in turn, and how each can be understood and acted on.

Detection

Detection takes the place of the more traditional location as the intention is that all the senses are used, not just the sight of what surrounds you and what you can see on the map. Use your ears and search for familiar sounds such as roads and railways that are marked on maps. Use a variety of 'clues' to determine your location.

[*] Sweetman, C. (2016) Land navigation - coaching concepts *Horizons* 73 pp32-35

The first mistake made by many when starting out in navigation is to look first at the map and then see what fits with what they can see around them. I suggest it is better to have a look round first, and use your ears and other senses to collect clues as to where you are. Then, with these clues in your mind, look at the map and match them to the image on the map. This avoids the bad (and wrong) habit of making the map fit what you can see, and convincing yourself that something is not there, or just can't be seen at the moment. Of course, on a trail centre route the observation should be relatively simple: finding the next way marker post. If you are in a forest or weather conditions mean you have little visibility, you need to replay what you have passed to help you 'see' where you have been. How many track junctions have there been? Are you going up or downhill? Steeply? Have you crossed or run by any streams? This is a skill learned and honed by going out to either a known location, or by close following of the route on the map and then looking and listening to determine what is around you, and how this matches what is on the map. How far can you see to realistically pick out details? How far is this on the map? Maybe over the fold?!

As you become more proficient in navigation it becomes smoother and faster, and soon you will be noticing the small details as a matter of course. To start with however, learning to navigate can be a pretty antisocial business as you spend your time with your head in the map or forcing yourself to notice details around you. If you are starting out it is best to do this foundation work on foot as the slower speed means you will be able to follow more easily where you are and continuously check the map without falling off or crashing.

Usually, with a little practice, this method of looking around you (and making sure your map is orientated so north on the map is north on the ground - use a compass for this), is good enough for detecting where you are in most situations. If you need some more detail, or this technique doesn't give you a clear idea, then think about looking for specific locations on the map and getting to them. Thus, you may not know exactly where you are at the moment, but relatively quickly you can get to an exact location, such as a path junction, or river crossing.

Moving on to more advanced skills you may find it necessary to triangulate your position, for which you will need a compass and at least two, preferably three known points on the map that you can see. These are often bigger landmarks, such as mountain peaks, churches (spires/towers are visually obvious across a landscape view, and marked clearly on OS maps) and major road junctions.

From your position, sight (look) along the edge of the compass so it is in a straight line to the object you are sighting on (the obvious landmark). Holding the compass still, pointing accurately at this landmark, turn the bevel (housing) until the North needle (usually red) is contained in the arrow drawn onto the housing. Subtract any magnetic variation needed for your location (see OS map sheets for this value - at time of writing in the UK this is so small as to be negligible, but in a few years will have changed as magnetic north

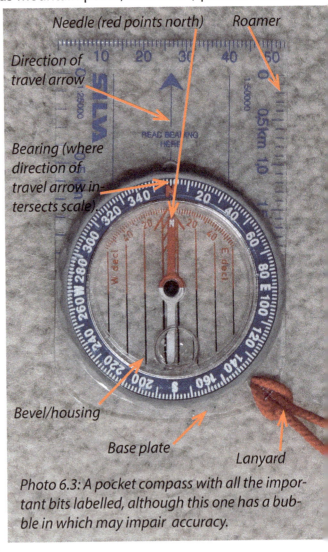

Photo 6.3: A pocket compass with all the important bits labelled, although this one has a bubble in which may impair accuracy.

is not a static position). Now lie the compass on the map with one edge running through the point you have just looked at (the landmark). Turn the map so that the North (red) needle points to the north on the map (almost always the top of the map). To be sure of accuracy line up the lines on the housing with the grid lines running vertically up and down the map (but turn the map not the compass housing). Your location is somewhere along this line - if you are on a path or road then wherever the line from your compass crosses the path/feature you are on, is where you are. If you are not on a linear feature like this, you will need to draw a line on the map with a pencil and repeat the process to a second landmark. Once you have two lines on the map you can be fairly sure where you are. Where the two lines cross is your location. If you want to be sure, or there is some concern that the landmark you have sighted off is not as obvious as you think (e.g. its a church spire but which church spire you're not sure), then repeat the process for a third time (hence triangulation) and you will be at the point where the lines cross. If they don't cross exactly (as is probable without using a specific sighting compass, then they will form a small triangle and you are located inside that area.

Destination

Once you have determined where you are by detection, you then need to consider your destination. This can be the ultimate destination, as when planning a route for a day/few hours' ride, or the next specific leg of the route you're following. Your destination should be somewhere you actually want to get to, as opposed to somewhere near where you want to go. Once you have established the destination, usually by looking at the map, you then need to plan how you will get there. This may be as simple as following a track/path, but may involve you working out changes in-direction caused by obstacles or inaccessible areas. You will also have to consider your priorities - the ease of the journey, speed of the journey or the interest of the group. For quicker journeys you would probably consider the shortest route to your destination, although this may involve going up and down hills so may be slower than you think. Of course the benefit of being on a bike is that after winching yourself up that steep hill you get to ride down the other side. If you're looking for that downhill thrill then you may purposefully go that way.

In order to make navigation to a set point easier, you may choose to aim at a really obvious feature that is close to your final destination and then get to the end point from there. This technique is known as aiming off, and involves navigating to an easy to identify point (path junction, fence crossing etc.) with a view to then travelling in one direction and picking up your actual end point from there. You will need to get as much information form the map as possible so that you don't overshoot your destination. Make a note (physically or mentally) of what you can expect to see at the end point. This is a particularly useful tip for mountain bikers as most people travel faster than they think they will so arrive at their destination sooner than expected - but don't overshoot it if they have a good idea what it looks like.

It may also be possible to follow a well defined feature to your destination, such as a stream or ridge line. This technique is known as hand lining or hand railing as you are using the feature as a hand line to guide you along your way. It is still very important to know what to expect when you get to the end point though.

Direction

Once you have your destination set, you need to know in which direction to travel. This may be as simple as following marked trails (such as at a trail centre), a set of features (track to a junction then turn left, then right at the edge of the forest etc.) or may require travelling on a bearing. Often you can see where you want to go, and this is a perfectly acceptable way of navigating. However if you can't see, or the route has direction changes then you may need to memorise a set of instructions (that you have worked out from the map) or use a bearing. A bearing is a mathematical measure of the angle you need to travel in, compared to magnetic north (as indicated by your compass, see photo 6.3).

Taking a bearing is really just the reverse of the procedure used for triangulation, explained in the detection section. To take a bearing from where you are (important to know this), lay your compass on the map with one edge on your position. Rotate the whole compass so that the straight line of the edge connects your position with your destination. Now, keeping the map and base plate of the compass still, turn the housing so that the lines on the housing and the drawn-on arrow (not the red needle) lie parallel with the vertical grid lines on the map i.e. the lines that run up and down. Lift the compass off the map and add on whatever magnetic variation applies for your area. You now have a bearing for where you need to go, and need to follow it to your destination. You do this by holding the compass and turning the whole thing so that the red needle (north) lines up with the arrow drawn onto the housing. Then move in the direction indicated by the direction of travel arrow. Remember that this will take you in a direct straight line to your destination, which is rarely an easy route as it may involve crossing streams, fences etc. It is useful to pick a point on the horizon or in the middle distance which is in line with your bearing and then travel to that so you don't have to have your head down all the time, which is nigh on impossible on a bike anyway.

Distance

When you have worked out where you want to go and in what direction it lies, you need to know how far away it is, including how much climbing or descending is involved. It you are travelling in a straight line it is fairly easy to measure this distance with the edge of the compass, which usually has a roamer etched/drawn on. More on the roamer shortly. If the route is not a straight line (as is often the case) you may need to use a little ingenuity to measure the distance. Do this by laying the lanyard along the route (starting at a knot or other sport on the lanyard that is clearly identifiable as where you started). Bend it and shape it so it matches as exactly as possible the actual route you will take, and mark on the end of the leg/section of route you are working on. Then lift this off of the map and lay it out straight next to the ruler or better, the roamer on the compass. Then you can measure the distance you will need to travel more easily.

The roamer is a marked set of numbers along on or both sides of the compass base plate. They are helpfully marked in units that relate directly to common map scales so you don't need to do any mathematical conversion to know how far you've measured. If you are working on a map to a scale not on the roamer then you will need to use the scale of the map to calculate the distance.

You can get an idea of the height you will gain or lose by looking at the contour lines marked on most maps. Check the vertical distance between them as this varied depending on the area, the map company and the scale of the map. They are marked at various intervals so you should be able to see if the direction is uphill or downhill (which obviously depends on the direction you are travelling too). Generally, contours close together mean steep slopes on the ground, and more widely spread contours indicate a shallow gradient. No contours or really widely spaced lines generally means a flat area, such as you might find along the bottom of a valley

Duration

The final concept to understand is the duration of the distance you will travel. The speed at which you travel will dictate how quickly you cover the ground, as will the ground and weather conditions. This is important when leading a group mountain biking as you need to know how long it will take to get to certain points - either so you can send the group off and get them to wait at suitable muster points, or so that you know how long you will be riding for before reaching your destination (either of the whole route or just that shorter section). Climbs tend to make you travel more slowly (especially if group members have to get off and push) and downhill sections tend to make you go faster.

In order to work out how long the route or section of a route will take you need to know how fast you're travelling. This is only ever going to be an estimate, as groups move at different rates according to many factors including group morale, expectation, competition within the group and obviously physical ability on a bike. If you are tracking your progress with a GPS device or a tracking app on your phone, such as Strava, you can usually access speed data in real time, so it should just take a glance. Generally a novice group riding off road for the first time will travel at about 9km/h on double track such as fire road or forest track. This will increase to about 12 or 13km/h on downhill within their ability, but will remain the same for anything too technical. They will climb at about 5km/h on a gradient which is not too steep to make them get off and push. If you're not sure of the speed that you are travelling, keep an eye on the time over the first few sections (hopefully you won't need to do so much detailed navigating early on in the ride) or even on the ride from the meeting point to the start of the route proper (the car park to the trailhead at a trail centre, for instance).

To work out how long the section will take to ride you need to divide the distance to be covered (in km not m) by the speed you will travel at (in Km/h). The result is the time it will take you in hours - but beware, as 1.2 hours is not 1 hour 20 minutes as time is not a decimal quantity. To find out the number of minutes relating to the number after the decimal point, take away the whole numbers (so in the example above, 1) and multiply what's left by 60 (so from above 0.2x60) which gives you the number of minutes. Thus, 1.2 hours is in fact 1 hour and 12 minutes.

As a rule of thumb, and keeping an eye on the time you are riding for, start to look out for your end of section markers/key features a few minutes before you should actually expect to get to them in case you have gone slightly faster than your calculations, and keep look for a few minutes after in case you've slowed down. If you haven't seen them after about 10 minutes further on than you expected, it will be a good idea to stop and check the map/GPS as you may have made a wrong turn or lost the route. Better to stop and check than ride out of your way for a long time, only to have to turn around and retrace your track!

A really useful tip to make sure you haven't overshot your mark is to look at the map a little way ahead of the intended end point and make a mental note of prominent features or obvious landmarks. That way if you are looking out for your end of section features but see these ones instead you know you have gone too far and need to retrace your track. These are known as check features and serve as a useful way to avoid going too far.

Photo 6.4: Waymarker posts at trail centres and on natural trails can show you the way to go and (as in the image on the left) what access rights exist to that particular route (see chapter 4 for more details.).

Preparation and planning

In preparing and planning your route, it is really important to pay attention to, and note down, the details of where you will ride. As already mentioned this is best done on paper and then as a pre-ride trip so that you are familiar with the navigational difficulties you may face and any terrain/access barriers. It is also useful to construct a route card of where you will go, especially if this is on natural trails and bridleways. At a trail centre it is usually enough to have a look at the trail map and a ride of the circuit to familiarise yourself. A route card also acts as a record to anyone who may be concerned if you are late back, or be tasked with calling out the emergency services if you don't re-appear within a reasonable time of your expected return. Its also really helpful for you if you have to evacuate from the route in an emergency, so you know where your escape routes are, and from where help can be summoned. An example route card is seen in figure 6.5, although there are many variations and you can create your own if you prefer to - whilst retaining the important information!

Further reading

For some more in-depth instruction in land navigation skills you may wish to have a look at the following:

Mountaincraft and Leadership - Eric Langmuir 4th Ed. Mountain training boards of England and Scotland, ISBN-10: 0956886906 ISBN-13: 978-0956886903

Navigation in the Mountains: The Definitive Guide for Hill Walkers, Mountaineers & Leaders - the Official Navigation Book for All Mountain Leader Training Schemes - Carlo Forte, UKMTB ISBN-10: 0954151151 ISBN-13: 978-0954151157

Hillwalking: The Official Handbook of the Mountain Training Walking Schemes - Steve Long 3rd Ed. Mountain training UK ISBN-10: 0954151194 ISBN-13: 978-0954151195

Figure 6.5: A sample MTB route card

Group Name		Leader and qualifications (if any)				Bikes used/hired from		Base contact			
Day number (if multi day)	Date	Start time	Group members + assistant(s) 1. 6. 2. 7. 3. 8. 4. 9. 5. 10.			General route location		Maps used			
Start GR	Distance	Estimate speed on section	Time Allowed for section	Time Added for stops and repairs	Estimated time of arrival at end of section	Route Description inc. end of section description		Emergency routes and nearest help			
To:											
To:											
To:											
To:											
To:											
To:											
To:											
Totals											

Air time, Mount Stromlo

7. What to Carry

> So what should you carry as a leader? What should each of your group carry as a minimum, if anything? Whilst this is a matter to be decided dependent on the group, the ride, the weather etc. this chapter contains a few essentials, along with some suggestions that may make your life easier on the trail.

Looking across Llyn Elsi, Gwydyr Forest, Snowdonia

What to carry

Whilst there are many factors which will affect exactly what you pack in your bag, there are a few essentials which you should never be without. As the leader you need to be able to look after yourself AND your group

A bag

It sounds like common sense, but it's important to carry a bag that can comfortably fit in all you need and be worn without impeding your riding. For a day ride, a 30 litre pack should be ample and you may be able to pare it down further. There are some great mountain bike specific designs out there, but a simple two pocket day-sack works fine. The straps should adjust so it can be snug around your shoulders and a waist/hip belt is needed to stop the bag moving as you ride. A chest strap is an optional extra that also helps in this regard.

A pump

As part of your pre-ride check you'll need to check tyres on all the bikes in your group, but invariably a puncture will happen some time. In this instance its vital you have a pump. A small pump that fits neatly

Photo 7.1: A general purpose 30 litre day-sack

> **Remember:**
> If you're using a bag with a pocket for a hydration bladder this often takes up quite a bit of space and can make it awkward to get at items nearer the bottom of your pack.

into your bag is a great investment, especially if it pumps air on both the in and out strokes (sometimes called a double pump). However, if you can manage to fit it in, a larger track pump makes inflating a tyre from flat much quicker. Spare tubes are also really useful to have either in your bag or somewhere on your bike. I keep one cable-tied to my stem for quick access and so it's one less thing not on my back.

Remember:
Make sure your pump can connect to Schrader and Presta valves, and any spare tubes are better to be Presta type so they fit in most rims.

Photo 7.2: Presta valve (left) and Schrader valve (right)

Tyre Levers

You'll need some tyre levers to get the tyre off the rim in order to replace a tube. Three is usually enough - most are made of plastic so that they don't damage alloy rims, but beware they can snap without warning (watch your knuckles on the spokes if this happens).

Photo 7.3: Plastic tyre levers

Cycle Spanner and Allen/Torx Keys

Many fittings on bikes are held by allen or torx bolts so a range of keys is essential for fixing things that work loose or come off during a ride. A multi-tool is an ideal way of carrying a selection of sizes without adding too much extra weight. A cycle spanner is still useful for things like pedals and acting as a large lever if you need it. Its also handy to have a few spare nuts and bolts of common sizes in your kit too, in case something comes off and gets lost.

Pliers/Cutters

These are useful if they are the same tool - you may need pliers to remove thorns or other items from a punctured tyre, or snip a cable-tie's end off. They are also useful for fixings that your cycle spanner doesn't fit, or for dealing with valves when they get stuck in the rim.

Gaffer Tape and Cable-ties

With a bit of ingenuity there's not a lot on a bike that you can't bodge with gaffer table and cable-ties - at least well enough to get you home, but don't rely on them for longer term fixes.

Tyre Boot

A section of old tyre a few inches long does a fine job of getting you home if the outer carcass of a tyre is seriously damaged. You can gaffer tape/cable-tie it over the problem area and then inflate the tube.

Chain Breaking Tool and spare links

Many multi-tools have a chain breaking tool incorporated, but it's important you know how to use it to both break, and re-join a chain. Spare links are useful if the chain gets mangled in a crash, as you can use them to replace damaged links without shortening the chain too much. Some chain breakers on multi-tools are quite small and don't give you the necessary leverage, so for leading a group its worth considering a specialist tool, as in photo 7.4. Alternatively you may need some chain braking pliers for chains that have a releasable link.

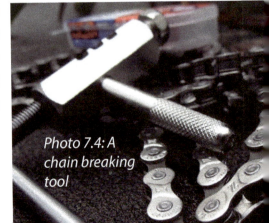

Photo 7.4: A chain breaking tool

Top Tip:
Carry a piece of old spoke about 10cm long which you've curved or bent into a hook at both ends. This can hook into chain links to take the tension of the chain whilst you're trying to rejoin links.

Photo 7.5: Old spoke hook taking chain tension

High-vis vest

At least two for road sections - one on the rider at the front (possibly you) and one for the rearmost rider.

Group Shelter

This can be a life saver in an emergency situation, keeping your group out of the elements whilst you administer first aid, or wait for rescue. In less serious situations it makes a cosy shelter for lunch too!

Photo 7.6: High vis vests are really important when riding on the road. At a minimum have one for the lead rider and one for the rider at the back. Ideally if you have more spread them throughout the group as can be seen here on the Long mynd, Shropshire.

Puncture repair kit

A bit old school, but worth having in case you use up all your spare tubes or really need to fix a puncture on the trail side. Make sure you know how to use it, and periodically check it's all ok as the rubber solution can either leak out or solidify if you're not careful with it. There are many brands available that come in small plastic boxes, ideal for stowing in a lid or side pocket of your bag.

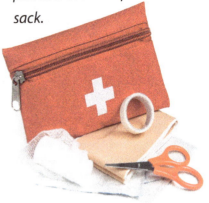

Photo 7.7: A first aid kit in a soft pouch is easier to pack in a rucksack.

First Aid Kit

Another obvious thing - but make sure it's big enough to cope with group situations and is dry and sterile (and all the sterile bits haven't gone out of date). More about the contents of your first aid kit can be found in chapter 9 - First Aid.

Torch

A small headtorch doesn't take up much space, but could be very important if you're lost or a mechanical problem keeps you out after dark.

Photo 7.8: Lightweight LED headtorches

Remember: Always carry spare batteries for your headtorch.

Map and Compass

Even if you know your route well, or are using a bike mounted GPS unit, always have a map and compass for backup (and know how to use them - see chapter 6 on navigation).

Photo 7.9: A group shelter in action (as a cosy lunch stop, that is)

Spare Gloves

As gloves are important safety gear, and have a habit of being put down and lost, its important to have some spares in case your group mislays one of theirs.

Mobile Phone

Although purists may want to enjoy the adventure and being out of touch with the wider world, it is a necessity when you're responsible for a group to have the means to summon help if needed.

Spare food/energy snacks

You may need these in an emergency, but they can also provide a morale boosting injection of sugar and energy if the group are becoming tired or dejected especially if the weather is bad.

Optional Extras

Depending on the time of year, the weather, the experience of the group, where you're riding etc. there are a few other things to think about putting in. You won't need all of the items all of the time, but sometimes they may come in handy.

- Sun cream
- Sunglasses/goggles
- Extra warm layers (for the group)
- Extra wind-proof layers (for the group)
- Buff or other neckwear
- Sleeping bag/bivvy bag/survival bag
- Guidebook
- Trail centre info booklet/leaflet
- Mosquito repellent
- High-vis vests - having several of these amongst the group is useful.

What your group should carry

Just as important as the gear you carry to support your group, are the things they each have with them so they can look after themselves. Again some of these items are weather dependent, but opposite is a list of the bare essentials that each rider should wear or carry.

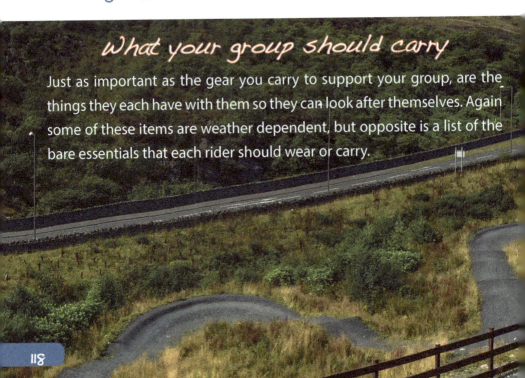

- A drink – enough to stay hydrated on the ride
- Some food – either a packed lunch for longer trips or some high energy snacks for shorter rides.
- Waterproof top – also acts as a windproof layer
- An extra warm layer – in case you have to stop for a mechanical or injury
- Any medication they know they may need – e.g. Asthma inhaler, Epipen etc.
- Hat and warm gloves – as with the spare layer in case you're forced to stop for a while.
- Headtorch – in case you're caught out and take longer than expected or if the weather closes in.
- Spare tube – on longer rides it makes sense if each rider has at least one themselves, and they don't take up that much room!

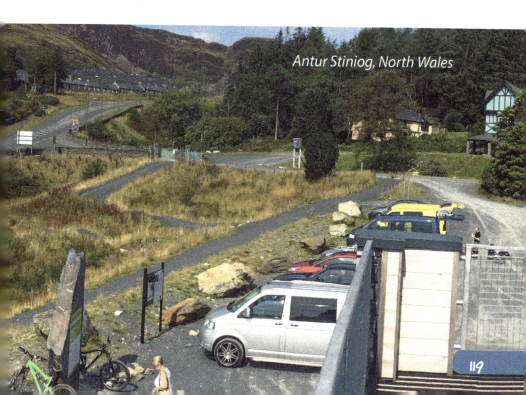

Antur Stiniog, North Wales

8. Know Your Bike

A damp day, Stanage Edge, Peak District

Before you lead a group, it's important to know something about the machines they're riding. Not just the make and model and any design specialities but the history, maintenance and what components they use. Using hired bikes brings the advantage of uniformity across the group but also the problem that hire bikes take a beating day in, day out, over a season and are sometimes fixed to keep them in operation as a priority. This chapter will help you identify common designs and components in order for those all important trail side repairs to be carried out quickly and without fuss.

Know your Bike
(and your group's bikes too!)

There are many designs out there - too many in fact to go into here, but there are a few general types and principles of design that most models follow with some small variations.

The most common bike you'll get from a hire shop or trail centre is a hardtail. These have front suspension and a solid rear end, the idea being to keep them light and simple - and most are just that - perfect for beginners or intermediate riders to hone their skills on. They're also pretty good for cross country racing and all day rides, and there's far less to go wrong on a multi-day expedition.

So, the main focus of this chapter is hardtails, with a short look at full suspension (full-sus) bikes. With these there are as many designs as there are bike manufacturers as some designs are or have been patented and ingenious designers have tackled the problem of a moving rear triangle differently! There are lots of ways the rear end is pivoted and bumps are absorbed; if you look out when you're riding you'll see plenty of variety.

Basic bike design

All bikes work on the same basic design of a big triangle up front and a smaller rear triangle. You sit above the join of the two triangles. Full suspension bikes allow the rear triangle to move in relation to the front triangle to smooth out bumps in the trail and keep the rear wheel in contact with the ground, giving you grip. They're great for downhill racing and are found on trail and all-mountain or enduro bikes, but have a disadvantage that there's more to go wrong/damage, and they also mean a weight penalty as the linkages, bolts and shock itself have to be accommodated. They also tend to cost more as there are more components involved.

Downhill Bikes

Downhill bikes (photo 8.1) tend to have a large coil spring around the shock to take the really big hits although there are some big hitting air shocks around now too. The coil springs allow the shock to control the really hard impacts encountered when going downhill really fast. The front of the bike is at a slacker angle too and the forks tend to have more travel too, again to take bigger hits. Forks also sometimes have a double crown - where the fork stanchions actually come past the bottom of the head tube and are braced across to the top of the steerer, giving a stronger design more able to take the hits. They tend to be longer and stable when going in a straight line, but much less manoeuvrable.

Trail and Enduro Bikes

Trail bikes can be hardtails or full-sus designs (see photo 8.2) and generally have a moderate to short amount of travel in the forks (120-150mm), with a fairly slack head angle, but not as slack as a downhill bike. The more eduro-focussed designs try to find the happy medium between a trail bike and a full on downhill rig. In other words something that is light enough to winch yourself up to the top of the hill but also fly down it. If there is a rear shock on the bike i.e. a full-sus design, it usually links the shock either vertically via a link attached to the seat post with the shock fixing to the join of the seat and down tube, or horizontally/parallel to the top tube with a similar link at the seat post (see photo 8.3 for an example). These bikes tend to have between 140 and 160mm of travel up front and are built to be as light as possible. They have a fairly slack head angle for downhill speed but compromise to allow them to be more agile than a downhill bike.

Hardtails

As previously stated, these are probably the most common bikes you will see, both at trail centres and in general. (The image in photo 8.4 which labels all the major parts of a mountain bike is a hardtail). They are also very common at hire shops. The reason for this abundance is simple - the less complex design and less need for expensive components makes them cheaper. Although there is a crossover between expensive hardtails and cheaper full-sus bikes (usually based on the construction/material of the frame and the specifications of the components), the simplicity of a hardtail has much to commend itself to the mountain bike leader. The advantages are in the simplicity of design (less to go wrong) and that there is less to set up correctly to ensure an enjoyable ride. Hardtails are often seen as an ideal starting platform to learn basic bike control and intermediate skills as there is a more direct feeling from the ground through the bike.

Components

Gear shifters

There are two types of gear shifter that you'll see - trigger shifters and twist or grip shifters. Trigger shifters are by far the most common, but there are some out there who prefer the grip shift, not least as it is less likely to get smashed in the event of a crash. They both adjust in much the same way - it's only when replacing a cable that there are differences.

Photo 8.1: A downhill bike - the Giant Glory Advanced 1

Photo 8.2 A full-sus enduro bike - the Yeti ASR

Photo 8.3: One of the many designs for rear triangle linkage - this one on a Santa Cruz Nomad C

Photo 8.4: A hardtail bike - the Rocky Mountain Vertex

Brakes

Brakes-wise you'll probably see disc brakes as standard now and almost all will be hydraulic (there are some cable disc brakes on cheaper models). Disc brakes offer much improved stopping power over traditional V or cantilever brakes, and you don't have to worry

Photo 8.5: A grip shifter

Photo 8.6: A trigger shifter

about them being less effective when its wet and muddy (which lets face it, is most of the time!)

Pedals

Photo 8.7: Hydraulic disc brakes

Pedals on hire bikes and most you see will be flat pedals designed to be ridden with any kind of shoe. The alternative is a clipless pedal where a cleat on the shoe fits into a spring loaded mechanism on the pedal (such as the Shimano SPD design - see photo 8.9). There are also hybrids about which are a clipless pedal with a flat platform around it to make clipping unnecessary for short sections and give greater stability to the rider's foot on the pedal (photo 8.9).

Seat posts and saddles

Seat posts and saddles are fairly similar in design, although you may see a dropper post on some higher end bikes, where the height of the seat post is controlled from the handle bars via a cable or hydraulic system and remote lever or button.

Photo 8.8 Cable disc brakes

Forks and shocks

Even the most basic suspension set-ups will have some form of lock out to firm up the suspension completely. More technical models will also have the options to adjust the compression (some have this as high and

Photo 8.9: MTB pedals - a hybrid clipless from Crank Brothers, an SPD clipless design from Shimano and a flat pedal from Redline

low speed controlled separately) and the rebound. These are usually controlled by wheels or knobs and most require a little time and testing to be set up properly.

Wheels and tyres

Wheels can be attached by thin QR skewers which need fit into thin U shaped drop outs, or more commonly now, bolt through axles with some form of quick release mechanism such as shown in photo 8.11. There are also three common wheel sizes, not to be confused. The original and older size is 26", still found on cheaper and older bikes. More modern bikes are likely to sport either 29" wheels (big wheelers) to help roll over smaller obstacles and boost efficiency when travelling longer distances, or 27.5/650b to try

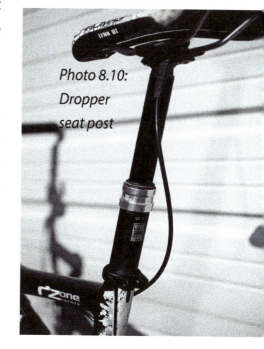

Photo 8.10: Dropper seat post

to harness the mile-munching abilities of big wheelers with some more manoeuvrability of the smaller 26" wheels.

There are also some newer sizes coming out known as 27.5+ and 29+, where the wheels are the size indicated by the numbers, but the rims are significantly wider to allow for wider tyres, in theory giving more grip. In practice a 27.5+ tyre and wheel combo is the same diameter as a normal 29" wheel so there are a few frame designs that offer the flexibility to swap between the two.

Finally you may also come across fat bikes (photo 8.12). These were originally designed for riding over snow or sand with tyre widths larger than 3". They have recently become popular at trail centres and you may see some riders on fat bikes when you're out with a group. They often have rigid forks as the extra air in the tyre can offer some cushioning, and tend to have more simple components as they are also designed to be lower maintenance for longer distance, more wilderness adventure type riding.

Photo 8.11: A quick release through-axle

Checking over the bike

Before each and every ride it's important to check the bike over, and if you're leading a group, get them to check their bikes to take some responsibility for their own machines. The M check, described below is a good way to remember what to check and you can go through this with a group quickly and efficiently with a group before each ride.

The M check

Start at the front wheel and check the wheel is securely held in place by either bolts (check pinch bolts too) or a quick release system. Check that the QR lever is facing up parallel with the fork stanchion. Move up to check the tyre is securely fitted and has enough pressure (you can use a

Photo 8.12: A fat bike in its natural element - this one a Surly Pugsley

pressure gauge if you have one). Lift the front wheel off the ground and spin it whilst looking down from above to look for any obvious bows or buckles (these may be fixed with some appropriate spoke tightening). Then check the headset is tight by holding the front brake on and gently rocking the bike forward against the resistance of the brake, whilst you run a finger round the headset at the top and bottom to feel if there is any movement. If there is you'll need to tighten up the headset.

Then move down the down tube and check the crank is securely attached and pedals are not loose. Move up the seat tube to check the saddle is securely held onto the seat post by the saddle rails and seat clamp. Check the seat post is appropriately attached too - if a dropper post or permanent fixing is used then it should be tight. If a QR seat clamp is used then it should be secure when closed and allow the seat post to slide when undone.

Finally move down the seat stays to the rear wheel where you need to check the tyre pressure, wheel alignment and attachment as with the front wheel. You should also check the rear mech (derailleur) by lifting the rear wheel from the ground and turning the pedals whilst changing gear. The mech should move one gear for each click of the shifter. Failure to do this may mean you need to adjust the tension in the cable. If one click moves the chain too far, i.e. more than one gear and the chain rattles against the cassette or the chain jumps two gears, then you need to loosen the cable and release tension. If the chain doesn't move far enough and hence won't change gear, you will need to tighten the cable by a quarter turn of the barrel at the shifter.

Common mechanical problems and trail fixes

Most modern mountain bikes are very reliable, and if you've done a thorough M check at the start of the ride, it is unlikely that there will be any problems. However, these are some common issues and how you can fix them well enough to get you back home, whilst on the trail. If you're leading a group, and a group member has the mechanical problem, you may need to give them your bike to get home whilst you ride the damaged bike back. This assumes your riding skills are of a higher level than the group you are leading.

The middle of nowhere - not a great place for a puncture!

Punctures

If a tyre goes flat, it has likely got a puncture. The quickest and easiest way to deal with this is just to replace the tube with one of the spares you're carrying. Remove the wheel and use the tyre levers to get the tyre off the rim, and then feel around inside the tyre with an un-gloved hand to check the puncture-causing object is not still lodged in the tyre. If it is remove it, and/or if there is an obvious hole in the tyre put some gaffer tape over the hole from the inside of the tyre before inserting the new tube. Take care around the valve as it is easy to pinch a new tube between the rim and the valve causing another puncture! Once you've got the tube in and the tyre back on, reinflate it and put the wheel back on the bike.
If you have a sidewall slash or a really big hole you may need to use a tyre boot (a section of old tyre) to cover over the outside of the tyre too. Make sure you cable tie and gaffer tape the section on as securely as possible - it won't look pretty but should get you home!

Buckled wheels

Wheels generally only buckle during a crash, but if this is the case you may be able to sort out a minor buckle with a spoke key. Leave the wheel on the bike and turn the bike upside down. Spin the wheel whilst looking directly down onto it and identify where the buckle is. Once you know where the buckle is you need to decide which way its bent. You need to tighten the spokes either side of the buckle that attach to the opposite side of the hub. You can also loosen the spoke where the buckle is. Only ever turn a spoke key a quarter turn at a time as a little movement translates to a lot of force and hence movement on the rim. If it is totally unfixable then you are going to end up walking.

Chain damage

If the chain breaks or gets damaged, you can use the chain breaker tool to shorten it and hence remove the damaged links. If you do this remember that you probably won't be able to use the largest cog on the cassette or the biggest cog on the front as the chain will no longer be long enough to cover them.

Front mech damage

If the front mech is damaged, the easiest way to get home is to slacken off the cable and avoid using it. You'll have to put the chain onto whichever size chain ring you want to use for the rest of the ride by hand, and then stick with it. Many modern trail bikes are 1x10 or 1x11 setups now so the front mech is becoming less popular anyway.

Rear mech damage

If the rear mech is bent, it may be possible to bend/bodge it back to shape or at least keep it serviceable for a few gears. If not then you're going to need to put the chain over the ring you want to use and stay in that gear all the way home - effectively turning your bike into a single speed. If you've really smashed up the rear mech then you'll need to break the chain and remove the mech altogether. If you do this you need to select the gear on the cassette you want to use, put the chain round it and then remove links from the chain until the chain is just tight enough around the cassette and front chain ring. Too tight and you'll snap the chain when it comes under load, too loose and it'll pop off the first time you go over a bump.

If you're following a route that involves significant distance or likely speed, it's worth carry a spare rear mech hanger as these are often designed to be sacrificed if the rear mech takes a serious knock. Many hire shops will supply you with a repair kit with hired bikes that often includes a spare mech hanger.

> **Top Tip:**
> Carry a piece of old spoke about 10cm long which you've curved or bent into a hook at both ends. This can hook into chain links to take the tension of the chain whilst you're trying to rejoin links.

Damaged saddles

Not common but one I've had to deal with is broken seat rails. Here creative cable tying and a lot of gaffer tape saved the day but definitely didn't look good! If dropper post mechanisms fail a couple of thick cable ties and gaffer tape can hold up the saddle. Dropper posts do come with a fixing collar in case this happens but very few riders (if any) who have a dropper will carry this with them.

Other problems

If anything else goes wrong then its really up to your creativity, and often how much gaffer tape and cable tie you can wind round or over something to get it to stay on. Ultimately if the mechanical has safety implications (such as a damaged brake) then you need to decide the safest way to proceed. It may be to give your bike to the person who's bike is damaged and ride the damaged one yourself. However, its really damaged beyond trail side repair then you'll need to walk out and /or put you emergency plan (discussed in chapter 1) into action.

> **Top tip:**
> It's worth carrying some different sized cable ties in your pack, not so much for the length as multiple ties can be joined together, but sometimes thicker ties are useful and sometimes you need thin ones.

> **Remember:**
> Always collect any broken parts or items you don't need. Firstly as it's good not to leave litter (see chapter 3) and secondly you may be able to fix things or get them to your LBS as opposed to having to buy expensive new parts once you've got home. It also helps to have a quick check round the area you've been working in to ensure you don't leave any tools behind.

Elan Valley, Wales

9. First Aid

Beddgelert Forest, Snowdonia

This chapter is no substitute for taking a specialist first aid course, but it covers some of the most common mountain bike related injuries, along with some special cases which are unusual unless you've had an accident on a bike. Taking an outdoor/adventure focussed first aid course is strongly recommended, but just in case the trainer hasn't come across some of these bike related specialities they're covered here.

First Aid

Mountain biking is perceived as a high risk sport. However, in terms of injuries sustained whilst riding as a member of a group with an appropriately qualified and experienced leader, there are actually significantly less incidents than for other adventure sports, such as rock climbing and white water kayaking.

The most common injuries are cuts, scrapes and grazes where people fall from their bikes. Occasionally these accidents happen at higher speed or the person falls awkwardly and there may be a broken wrist, arm or collar bone as a result of putting out the arms to arrest a fall. Head injuries are not that common as your group members should all be wearing helmets, although this does not prevent concussion from a serious impact (but should reduce the risk of skull fracture). In extreme cases if the bike is damaged or the person collides with a solid/sharp object there may be puncture wounds (e.g. from spokes) or impalements (e.g. from sharp branches), long lacerations or facial injuries involving eyes and teeth.

This chapter covers how to deal with most of these injuries, but it is **no substitute for a first aid course**. Most (if not all) of the leadership qualifications available require a valid first aid certificate in order for the leadership qualifi-

> *Remember:*
> *Always check your first aid kit is topped up with in-date supplies before you go out on the ride.*

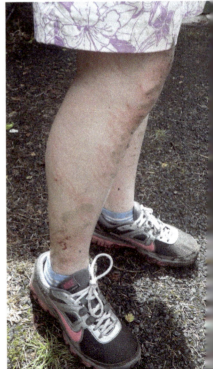

Photo 9.1: A grazed knee and lower leg caused by a fall at low speed.

cation to be valid. This chapter is therefore not going to cover things such as unconscious casualties, serious head injuries or medical problems such as heart attacks. For those you need to **read a proper first aid manual and go on a certified first aid course!**

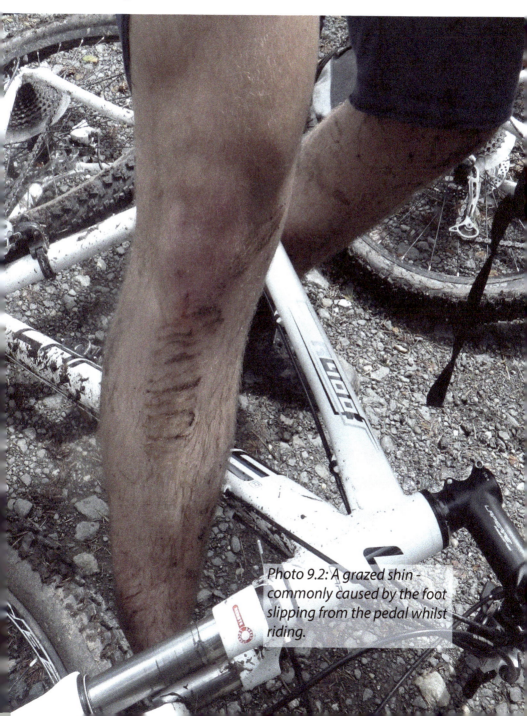

Photo 9.2: A grazed shin - commonly caused by the foot slipping from the pedal whilst riding.

> **Remember**
> In any incident which looks like it may require first aid, it is important you ensure the safety and well-being of the rest of your group before you treat the injured party(ies). This includes making sure you are not putting yourself in any danger by treating the casualty. Often this will be as simple as getting your group together, off their bikes and off the trail. If you think you may need longer than a few minutes then it is worth telling the group to put on their extra warm layer that they've brought, (see chapter 7) and/or getting them into the group shelter (it's also easier to treat your casualty in the group shelter if the weather is bad).

Photo 9.3: A grazed arm which will need cleaning!

Grazes and cuts

Grazes of all sorts usually need to be cleaned as gently as possibly to remove traces of grit and dirt from them. This may not be possible to do thoroughly by the trail, but you can use either the sterile wipes or sterile water/saline solution in your first aid kit for the purpose. If there is a small amount of bleeding then a plaster will suffice as a barrier to further ingress of dirt, but the wound will need re-examining and another clean once you get back to base/home. It is possible to prevent some grazes by wearing appropriate padding to the knees and elbows, or by wearing long trousers and long sleeves. However it is unlikely that a beginner level rider would have knee/arm pads and long sleeves/trousers can be warm and cumbersome, so it is worth briefing your group on the risks so they can make their own choices (if appropriate).

Cuts can be a bit more serious and you may need to apply some direct pressure to stem any bleeding. Generally it's a good idea to try to raise the bleeding limb above the heart to slow blood flow, so the injured rider may need to lie down. If the cut is bigger, or deeper than can be managed with a plaster, then apply a sterile dressing. The problem you have here is that if the limb with the cut needs to be moved or bent to continue, the cut will probably open up under the increased pressure of blood flow due to movement. If you have a cut this serious you will probably need to consider putting your emergency action plan into action and consider evacuating the injured person.

> **Top Tip:**
> A couple of tubes of sterile water are far easier to use to clean out a graze than sterile wipes. Although the job can be done with wipes there is a risk of pushing any grit or dirt into the wound. Sterile water can also be used effectively for eye injuries as well.

Fractures

Fractures or suspected fractures should be treated cautiously and carefully, as ideally they should not be moved. Obviously this has to be done with a modicum of common sense and a judgement of risk of leaving them where they are. Fractures to arms and collar bones can be supported using a sling (elevated for collar bone, low sling for lower arm injuries), and it is very unlikely that the rider will be continuing. Thus, help will need to be summoned or a walk back to base or the emergency escape route (see chapter 1) followed. If you don't have enough triangular bandages to immobilise the limb, then improvise - spare tubes and gaffer tape can be made to act in place of bandages if they are there to keep the limb still.

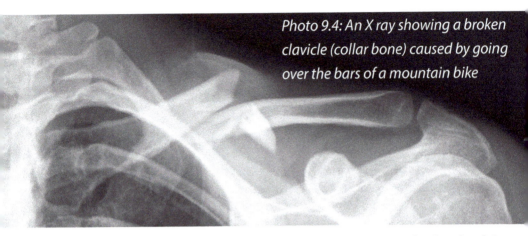

Photo 9.4: An X ray showing a broken clavicle (collar bone) caused by going over the bars of a mountain bike

If you have to treat a fracture, it is worth treating the casualty for shock in case there is any internal blood loss that you can't see. If you're at a trail centre then a call to the centre itself will mean some form of help can be mustered, even if it's a vehicle to get you back to the car park and then hospital. If you're out on natural trails then you need to get to a point where the emergency services can get to you or call them out directly to your position if your casualty is unable to move. A suspected fracture will always need to go to hospital to get checked out by a medical professional.

> **Top Tip:**
> When immobilising a fracture/tying a sling, let the casualty put it in the most comfortable position themselves before you start trying to immobilise it.

Concussion/blows to the head

Head injuries should be taken seriously, even if they appear to be inconsequential at the time. Even a bang on the head protected by a helmet can cause concussion if it is a hard enough impact. If the rider feels nauseous or is sick, or has blood from their ears or eyes, then you should suspect a fracture to the skull and call the emergency services as soon as possible, while monitoring your casualty. Treatment for concussion would ideally involve discontinuing the ride and being monitored for 24 hours as well as a trip to hospital to ensure there are no other injuries caused by the blow to the head. In practice if the only practical way to help is to continue, you should watch the injured person carefully and support them whilst they are walking - as a blow to head can cause problems with vision and balance. Riding on is not recommended as they may misjudge another obstacle, or lose balance at a crucial time, thus having another accident and potentially another injury. If in doubt call the emergency services.

Facial injuries

Facial injuries should also be treated with caution as they are part of the head. Particular care should be taken of eyes if they are damaged. As with any other bleeding wound pressure and dressings should be applied, but if the damage is the eye itself it is worth bandaging both eyes, as your binocular vision will often cause the injured eye to continue move and try and focus even under a dressing, which could exacerbate the original injury.

Photo 9.5: Sometimes a fall over the bars can result in a serious facial injury - in this case it was just a muddy graze and some wounded pride.

Teeth that get knocked out should be collected where possible and kept clean and cool (in water or milk) pending a trip to the dentist. Again a blow to the jaw causing dental problems is still a head injury, so you would be wise to suspect concussion and treat accordingly.

Impalements/Objects in wounds

When someone has an accident there is the rare chance that some part of them will become impaled on either a part of the bike or an object in the near area. Most bits of bikes are not that sharp and would probably break before piecing the skin, but it is possible that a spoke could puncture a person, and I've attended (as a first aider) an incident where someone had a brake lever impaled in their arm. More common is for riders to get bits of sharp rock like slate or volcanic glass stuck quite deeply into them when riding (and then falling) on terrain containing such rocks.

In any impalement situation, the key thing is not to remove the item sticking into the person. If you remove it there will almost certainly be some serious bleeding as there will be a hole where the item was. If possible put pressure around the object to prevent any further blood loss. If you cannot move the injured person without moving the impaling object, then as long as it will not cause further harm, leave them be and call the emergency services. If you absolutely have to move them, try to keep the object in the wound still as you move them. If it were say a broken spoke sticking into a leg, try to cut the spoke off fairly close to the wound (not flush with it so that the medical professionals have something to pull on to remove it), but so that there is less of a lever to get knocked and cause further pain and injury.

Across the dam, Elan valley, Wales

Remember

Do a first aid course!

(Preferably one focussed on outdoor adventure sports and the wilderness, covering rescue and emergency care.

10. Conclusion

So what now? You've read the book and hopefully picked up some tips along the way, and perhaps seen an aspect of mountain bike leadership you hadn't yet considered. This final chapter aims to tie everything together so you can get out there and lead your group in a safe, enjoyable and sustainable mountain biking adventure.

Glendalough, Co. Wicklow, Ireland

Conclusion

So how to end a book containing such a variety of different topics? I hope you've learned something new as a result of reading this, and perhaps it will help you have more effective and most importantly more enjoyable sessions out when you are leading groups - whether that's paying clients or a group of mates.

Since I started writing this book even more trail centres have opened up, making mountain biking ever more accessible so I would strongly urge you to pass on what you know and love about being out on your bike to other people.

This book has set out the principles and practices of what I believe make an effective leader. In the first chapter I covered the sorts of behaviours and characteristics that I expect to see when I'm assessing people for one of the mountain bike leadership awards. Then in chapter 2 we got into some fairly deep stuff concerning coaching, teaching and how this all fits in to the role of a mountain bike leader. Chapter 3 gave a brief insight into how to be more sustainable as a leader in what is perceived as a fairly de-

The briefing before the ride, Anglesey

structive activity, and chapter 4 looked at how and where you can actually ride your bike, off-road. Chapter 5 covered a bunch of skills that you will need to use at some point or another on the trail, and aimed to give details so that even if you can't do it yet, with some practice you should be able to. The idea here is also to give you a mental picture so that when you're coaching and teaching others you have a correct version to compare things to. Chapter 6 looked at knowing where you are and how to get where you want to go, especially if you choose the more adventurous riding to be had on bridleways and byways that crisscross the country side. Chapter 7 set out what you should be carrying as a leader so you know the sorts of things to pop in your pack, and what your group members should also be carrying. Chapter 8 lead on to how to look after a bike particularly on the trail, with some trail side tips and fixes, before chapter 9 brought on the spectre of dealing with injuries to riders not bikes.

So there you - go a whistle-stop tour of mountain biking. There is so much more out there to discover, in particular the enjoyment of sharing your fun and rewarding experiences with others.

If you want to know more then I recommend you look into one of the leadership awards offered by British Cycling or the Mountain Bike Instructor Award Scheme. Yes, that's right there is no one national governing body for mountain biking so it can appear daunting to know where to look at first. However, I hold strongly to the conviction that variety is the spice of life, and the various awards allow you to lead and coach in different ways and in different environments and contexts, so there really is something out there for everyone. Have look online for mountain bike leader awards as the two awarding organisations mentioned are but two of quite a few.

Whatever you do, keep on pedalling and enjoy the ride.

See you on the trail!

Index

A

Access iii
  Ordnance Survey 50
  Rights of way 50
    byways open to all traffic 51
    public bridleways 51
    public footpaths 51
    road used as a public path 51
  Trail centres 54
    Riding the trails 56
    Sessioning a section 57
    Skills development areas 58
Allen/Torx Keys 113

B

bag 112
bike design 122
British Cycling 149
Buckled wheels 133

C

Cable-ties 114
Chain Breaking Tool 114
Chain damage 133
Coaching iii
  coach behaviours 26
  Coaching 20
  coaching and teaching. 20
  Coaching competencies 22
  Delivery or intervention 24
  Demonstrating 36
  direct intervention approach 26
  Duration 24
  Feedback 33
  learning styles 27
  Observation and analysis 28
    Analytical 29
    Deductive 29
    Holistic 29
  Participation incentive 24
  pedagogy 20
  Planning 24
  practice 31
  Questioning 31
  Reasons 24
  The coaching process 23
  verbal instructions and commands 38
Components 124
  Brakes 128
  Dropper seat post 129
  Forks 129
  Gear shifters 124
  Pedals 128
  quick release through-axle 130
  Seat posts and saddles 128
  shocks 129
  tyres 129
  Wheels 129
Cycle Spanner 113

D

Downhill Bikes 122

E

Enduro Bikes 123
Environmental Impact iii
  Access restrictions 47
  berms 45
  braking bumps 44
  erosion 42
  Litter 46
  Noise 46

Plant life 47
skid 44

F

fat bikes 130
First Aid iii
  blows to the head 142
  Concussion 142
  cuts 138
  Facial injuries 143
  First Aid Kit 116
  Fractures 141
  grazes 138
  Grazes and cuts 140
  Impalements 143
  scrapes 138
Front mech damage 134

G

Gaffer Tape 114
group shelter 117
Group Shelter 115

H

hardtail 126
Hardtails 123
High-vis vest 115

L

Leadership iii
  being a leader 4
  CLAP 13
  generic responsibilities 8
  Leadership styles 7
  Meeting the group 10
  Preparation and planning 10
  Responsibilities of a leader 6
  Riding on the road 14
  risk benefit analysis 8

Road crossing 16
  The filter crossing 16
  The gated crossing 16
Roles of a leader 4
Sections of technical difficulty 12
Styles of leadership 5

M

M check 130
Mobile Phone 117
Mosquito repellent 118
Mountain Bike Instructor Award
    Scheme. 149
mountain bike leadership awards
    148

N

Navigation iii
  compass 100
  Destination 101
  Detection 98
  Direction 102
  Distance 103
  Duration 104
  Five D's of Land Navigation 98
  GPS 97
  Navigation technology 95
  roamer 104
  route card 108
  Taking a bearing 103
  Trail centre navigation 97
  triangulate your position 100
  Waymarker posts 106

P

Pliers 114
Presta valve 113
pump 112
Punctures 133

R

Rear mech damage 134
repair kit 116
Riding skills iii
  Berms 82
  Bike set up 62
  Boardwalk riding 76
  Braking 66
  Bunnyhop 89
  Carrying your bike 88
  Cut outs 87
  Doubles 73
  drop offs 79
  Drop offs 87
  Flowing singletrack 72
  Front wheel lift 78
  Gear selection 64
  log hopping 76
  Northshore 88
  off camber 71
  riding a double and pumping for speed 75
  Riding downhill 69
  Riding uphill 68
  Rocky sections 84
  Rollers 72
  Rooty sections 81
  Rutted tracks 80
  Steep slopes 86
  Table tops 84
  Track stand 67
  Water crossing 80

S

Schrader valve 113
Spare food 117
Spare Gloves 117
Sun cream 118

T

Torch 116
Tyre Boot 114
Tyre Levers 113

W

What to Carry iii

Lightning Source UK Ltd.
Milton Keynes UK
UKHW022351220719
346619UK00008B/48/P